Vagueness and the Evolution
of Consciousness

Michael Tye is the Dallas TACA Centennial Professor in Liberal Arts at the University of Texas at Austin. He has taught at Temple University, St Andrews, and King's College, London. His main area of interest is consciousness, and he has also written on mental imagery, the nature of thought, and vagueness.

Vagueness and the Evolution of Consciousness

Through the Looking Glass

MICHAEL TYE

OXFORD
UNIVERSITY PRESS

Great Clarendon Street, Oxford, OX2 6DP,
United Kingdom

Oxford University Press is a department of the University of Oxford.
It furthers the University's objective of excellence in research, scholarship,
and education by publishing worldwide. Oxford is a registered trade mark of
Oxford University Press in the UK and in certain other countries

© Michael Tye 2021

The moral rights of the author have been asserted

First published 2021
Firstpublishedinpaperback2023

Published in the United States of America by Oxford University Press
198 Madison Avenue, New York, NY 10016, United States of America

British Library Cataloguing in Publication Data
Data available

Library of CongressCataloginginPublicationData
Data available

ISBN 978-0-19-886723-4 (Hbk.)
ISBN 978-0-19-889295-3 (Pbk.)

Contents

Introduction   1

1. A Paradox of Consciousness   4
   1.1 The Paradox Explained: Part A   6
   1.2 The Paradox Explained: Part B   13

2. Russellian Monism to the Rescue?   19
   2.1 Versions of Russellian Monism   24
   2.2 Objections to Reductive Russellian Monism   25
   2.3 Objections to Primitivist Russellian Monism   28
   2.4 A Final Concern   31

3. Transparency and Representationalism   32
   3.1 The Transparency Thesis   32
   3.2 Qualia Realism   34
   3.3 Two Arguments from Transparency Against
       Qualia Realism   35
   3.4 How Does Transparency Support Representationalism for
       Visual Experience?   39
   3.5 Blur   41
   3.6 Extending Transparency: Bodily Sensations   43
   3.7 Emotions and Moods   48
   3.8 Conscious Thoughts   55
   3.9 More on Property Representationalism   58
   3.10 Objections and Clarifications   62
   3.11 An Argument for Property Representationalism   69
   3.12 Moore and the Missing Ingredient   71

4. Representationalism and Panpsychism   73
   4.1 The Problem of Undirected Consciousness   75
   4.2 The Problem of Combination   80
   4.3 Poise and the Global Workspace   85
   4.4 More on the Problem of Combination   88
   4.5 The Problem of Tiny Psychological Subjects   91
   4.6 The Causal Efficacy of Consciousness   93

5. The Location of Consciousness 100
  5.1 A Hypothesis by Crick and Koch 100
  5.2 Decorticate Children 103
  5.3 The Prefrontal Cortex and Working Memory 105
  5.4 Where in the Animal Realm Is Consciousness Located? 107

Bibliography 117
Index of Names 127
Index 129

Introduction

As you may recall, when Alice stepped through the mirror, she encountered a very peculiar world in which many of the people she met were chess pieces or characters from nursery rhymes. Everything was inside out, upside down. So it is with consciousness.

Reflection upon the appearance of consciousness in living beings suggests that there are just two alternative views. Either consciousness appeared suddenly so that its appearance is like that of a light switch being turned on or it arose through intermediate stages, not yet definitely involving consciousness but also not definitely not involving it. On the former view, consciousness is an on/off matter, but once it arose, it became richer and richer through time rather as a beam of light may become brighter and broader in its sweep. On the latter view, consciousness is not an on/off matter. There are shades of gray. There is no one moment at which consciousness appeared. It arose gradually just as life did, becoming richer through time as animal brains became more complex.

The latter view seems more plausible at first glance; for if consciousness suddenly appeared out of the blue, as it were, then what was responsible for its sudden emergence? Presumably the occurrence of some suitable neural state. But neurological states themselves admit of borderline cases, so the relevant neural state cannot itself have arisen suddenly. Instead it must have appeared gradually through various intermediate neurological stages. So, if consciousness originally appeared suddenly without any borderline cases, it cannot be identified with any such neurological state; nor for similar reasons can it be identified with any complex functional or informational state supported by the neurological architecture. It seems, then, that if consciousness appeared suddenly, it must be something special and new, totally different from the physical properties of the underlying neural and functional architecture. But if this is the case, what could consciousness be? It appears that we are driven to think of consciousness as something nonphysical in nature that suddenly emerged in certain animal brains without any further explanation. This is very hard to accept.

On the other hand, if consciousness arose gradually then we should be able to describe borderline cases of consciousness just as we can for life. Unfortunately, as I shall argue, that we cannot do. Putative borderline cases of consciousness are all cases in which there is indeterminacy in *what* is experienced, and not in experience or consciousness itself. So, a kind of paradox arises. Consciousness cannot be sharp or precise, but equally it cannot be vague.

The paradox is laid out fully in the first chapter. One possible response to this paradox is to say that it is based on a mistaken assumption about the origins of conscious states. Conscious states did not arise with neurological complexity. Instead, they are fundamental features of microphysical reality (panpsychism) or at least they are grounded in such fundamental features. Chapter 2 lays out the standard version of this view: Russellian Monism. I argue that the view, in either of its two standard elaborations, faces overpowering objections.

In the next two chapters, I discuss the relationship between conscious states and consciousness itself. I argue that the basic tenet of the representationalist view of conscious states can be preserved within a framework that takes consciousness itself, or rather a central element of consciousness I call "consciousness*", to be sharp but conscious states vague. Consciousness*, I claim, is indeed a fundamental feature of micro-reality, and thus it did not evolve, but conscious states are not. Conscious states evolved gradually, as did life, through a range of borderline cases. The view with which I end up presents novel solutions to three important problems (the problem of undirected consciousness, the problem of combination, and the problem of tiny, psychological subjects). It also takes up the question of how consciousness can be causally efficacious with respect to animal behavior.

That I am prepared to embrace a position that has something in common with the panpsychist world view will come as a surprise to many, given my past writings on consciousness, but as John Perry quipped: "If you think about consciousness long enough, you either become a panpsychist or you go into administration," and I haven't gone into administration. I cannot say that the transition has been an easy one. But, to repeat, I am still a representationalist about consciousness. I am also still a physicalist. And it is consciousness*, not consciousness, I maintain, that is to be found in the micro-realm. So, the change is not quite as radical or dramatic as it may first seem.

Chapter 5 turns to the question of where in the brain macro-consciousness is located and which animal brains so evolved as to support conscious states. It is suggested here that even though conscious states appeared gradually, on the account I am offering, it may well be true that in human brains and those of many other species, there is a trigger for conscious states that *typically* (though not always) turns such states on or off and so functions in the same general way as a light switch.

The world is a strange place, if you look into it deeply enough, not as far removed from the world Alice encountered through the looking glass as lay people suppose. We know that already from theories in physics which tell us that microphysical entities are both waves and particles, that there can be action at a huge distance (one so great that there cannot be a causal connection, as in quantum entanglement), and that time is dependent on a frame of reference. Perhaps it is only fitting that consciousness should turn out to be strange too.

I am grateful to audiences at talks in the USA, the UK, and China for comments and discussion. I would like to thank specifically Derek Ball, Zack Blaesi, Paul Boghossian, Jane Chen, David Chalmers, Alex Grzankowski, Keith Hossack, Cheyenne Howell, Jon Litland, David Papineau, Simon Prosser, Connor Quinn, Mark Sainsbury, Henry Shevlin, and Jonathan Simon. I am also indebted to two referees for Oxford University Press, who gave me much food for thought in their detailed reports.

1

A Paradox of Consciousness

Some philosophers and scientists have likened the appearance of consciousness in living beings to that of a light switch being turned on. Consciousness, on this view, suddenly appeared and then it became richer and richer through time rather as a beam of light may become brighter and broader in its sweep (see, for example, Searle 1992). On such a picture, either consciousness is present or it isn't. There are no shades of gray. But once consciousness has emerged, there are different degrees of consciousness.

Others have said that the light switch model for consciousness is fundamentally misconceived. Consciousness is *not* an on/off matter. Rather consciousness arose gradually just as life did (see, for example, Lycan 1996; Dennett 2004). Advocates of this view deny that consciousness is an all-or-nothing phenomenon, even in our own case.

One way to put the disagreement here is in terms of vagueness. Typically vagueness is understood in terms of borderline cases. Here are some representative quotations:

> However borderline cases should be characterized, it is a datum that vague concepts give rise to them. (Wright 2003, p. 93)

> It is better to define a predicate as vague if and only if it is capable of yielding borderline cases, where the notion of borderline cases is introduced by examples. (Williamson 1994, p. 171)

> What does it mean to say that 'bald' is vague? Presumably it means that the predicate admits borderline cases. (Field 1994, p. 410)

Notice that in the above quotations, predicates and concepts are classified as vague. This is part and parcel of the common view that vagueness is ultimately a linguistic or conceptual phenomenon. But we can also sensibly ask whether, for example, the property of being bald or the property of being red admit of borderline cases and are thereby vague. And the answer to these questions seems clearly 'yes'. The boundary between red and orange is fuzzy. Objects having a color in that region are neither definitely red nor definitely not red, and so are borderline red. Likewise, some people with small patches of hair on their head do not have sufficiently few hairs to count as definitely bald but then neither are they definitely not bald. They are in the gray area.

We can now put the disagreement about consciousness in terms of the following question. Is consciousness like being bald and being red in being *vague*, that is, in allowing borderline cases or is consciousness like being an even number in being *sharp*, that is, in not being capable of having borderline cases? Searle holds that consciousness is sharp, as do McGinn (1982), and Simon (2017).[1] Dennett and Lycan hold that consciousness is vague as does Papineau (2002) and as did I previously (Tye 1996).

There is one further point of clarification needed. Consciousness, for present purposes, is experience. Experiences are mental states such that there is inherently something it is like subjectively to undergo them. Examples are feeling pain, feeling an itch, visualizing an elephant, experiencing anger, and feeling fearful. In each of these cases, it is incoherent to suppose that the state exists without there being some phenomenology, some subjective or felt character. Thus to say that a state is conscious in the present context just is to say that it is an experience; and to consider whether consciousness is vague is to consider whether there can be borderline cases of experience.

In understanding the term 'consciousness' in this way, I do not mean to suggest that the term has not had other uses both in science and philosophy. Sometimes, for example, it is held that a mental state is conscious just in case it is one of which its subject is introspectively aware. This is sometimes called 'higher-order consciousness'. My claim is simply that among the various mental states we undergo, many of which are introspectively accessible (but arguably not all), are experiences and feelings, and these states, unlike beliefs, for example, are inherently such that they *feel* a certain way. Different experiences differ in how they feel, in their subjective character, and that is what makes them different experiences. In being this way, experiences are conscious mental states by their very nature. This point is sometimes put by saying that experiences are *phenomenally* conscious.[2]

---

[1] Antony (2006) has a complex view which allows that consciousness may turn out to be vague even though our current concept of it is sharp. More on this below, pp. 19–20.
[2] In various places in this book, I adopt this usage myself.

The paradox I wish to discuss is a paradox about phenomenal consciousness. It can now be stated as follows:

1) Consciousness is either sharp or vague.
2) If consciousness is sharp, then it isn't a (broadly) physical phenomenon.
3) Consciousness is a (broadly) physical phenomenon.
4) *Consciousness is vague* (from 1, 2, 3).
5) If consciousness is vague, then there are possible borderline cases of consciousness.
6) There are no possible borderline cases of consciousness.
7) *Consciousness is not vague* (from 4, 5, 6).
8) *Consciousness is both vague and not vague* (from 4, 7).

A contradiction!

1.1 The Paradox Explained: Part A

Premise (1) of the paradox is an instance of the logical law of the excluded middle. Either consciousness is sharp or it is not sharp, that is, it is vague. Premise (2) is sometimes taken to be an obvious, nonlogical truth. Colin McGinn, for example, says:

> Whatever the explanation [of the all-or-nothing character of consciousness] is—whether indeed the all-or-nothing character of consciousness can be explained—this seems to be a feature that any account of consciousness must respect. And there are theories of the mind, such as materialism and behaviorism, that will find this feature problematic, since the concepts in terms of which they choose to explain mental phenomena do not exhibit this all-or nothing character. (1982, p. 14)

This seems to me too fast; for why should we accept that *all* the concepts available to the physicalist for giving an account of mental phenomena are vague? (2) is surely better based on a consideration of the various alternatives open to the physicalist about the nature of consciousness.

Consider first the type identity theory and the hypothesis put forward by Crick and Koch that consciousness is one and the same as neuronal oscillation of 40MHz. It is evident that Crick and Koch did not intend this hypothesis to rule out every neuronal oscillation that is not *exactly* 40MHz.

What about a neuronal oscillation of 40.1 MHz? Or 40.01MHz? Or 40.000001 MHz? Their proposal is that consciousness is one and the same as neuronal oscillation of *approximately* 40MHz or neuronal oscillation *sufficiently* close to 40MHz. But these formulations of the hypothesis bring out its inherent vagueness, and not just from the use of the terms 'approximately' and 'sufficiently'; for the term 'neuron' is vague too.

Neurons are complex physical entities with diverse components. Each neuron has a cell body, dendrites, and an axon. Electrical impulses come in along the dendrites and go out along the axon. Imagine removing atoms one by one from a given neuron. Eventually, as one does so, there will be no neuron left. But along the way, there will surely be a range of borderline cases—entities that are neither definitely neurons nor definitely not neurons. So, the property of being a neuronal oscillation is vague. It admits of borderline cases. In general, neurophysiological properties are highly complex. The idea that the relevant neural properties for consciousness are sharp is extremely implausible.

What about representational or functional role or behavioral properties? The proposal that there cannot be borderline cases here is again very implausible. Borderline cases of representational properties are easy to specify. Take the property of representing *meat*. Historically, the word 'meat' meant *being edible*: through time, it came to mean *being flesh*. It is very hard to accept that the transition was sudden. More plausibly, there was a gradual drift and thus a period of time at which the word neither definitely meant one nor definitely meant the other. This was not *because* being edible and being flesh are vague (though they are). Rather it is because the property of representing itself admits of borderline cases. For a nonconventional example, consider a neuron in the visual cortex, the firing of which represents the presence of an edge. Natural representation is usually taken to be a matter of tracking under normal conditions. Since the concept of normality is vague if it is cashed out statistically (what *typically* happens) and also vague if it is understood teleologically (what is *supposed* to happen if the relevant system is operating properly), natural representation is vague too.

Turning to functional role properties, there are physical inputs and outputs and these will admit of borderline cases whether they are at the level of activity on sensory and motor neurons or at the level of environmental inputs and behavioral outputs. Furthermore, functional role properties are properties that involve *normal* conditions, so the points just made with respect to natural representation carry over. Similar points apply to any direct appeal to behavioral properties.

So far, then, it seems that if consciousness is taken to be a broadly physical phenomenon, it is vague, as premise (2) asserts. But perhaps there are further plausible physical candidates for identification with consciousness that aren't vague, candidates not to be found in neurophysiology or functional roles or behavior or representation. Might such candidates be found within microphysics? Once again, this is implausible. We are conscious; rocks and plants are not. But if we are physical beings, then we and rocks and plants are built of the same basic stuff. So, why are we conscious and rocks and plants not?

The obvious answer is that we have brains. Consciousness requires a brain. So, the relevant physical properties, if any there be, for identification with consciousness should be of a sort found in neurophysiology or in functioning or representation at a level of complexity that requires a brain. And such complex properties I have argued are not sharp.

Perhaps it will now be suggested that we should look to the *chemistry* of brain processes for the relevant physical properties. Take the feeling of anxiety, for example. That is associated with a decrease in serotonin and dopamine levels in the brain. Again, however, inevitably vagueness will arise. How large a decrease in serotonin and dopamine? To put a numerical value on the decrease is to invite the response that a very tiny amount more or less would surely not make a difference. To say that the decrease must be sufficiently large is to introduce vagueness right away. It is also worth noting that the appeal to decreased serotonin and dopamine *in the brain* brings vagueness with its use of the qualifier "in the brain"; for the brain lacks sharp boundaries and so there are borderline cases of changes *in* the brain. It does not help to drop the qualifier "in the brain," I might add, since serotonin is produced widely throughout the body, but it is only the serotonin that is produced in the brain that matters directly to feelings. There is no reason to think that these points are not applicable to consciousness generally.

Suppose it is now proposed that integrated information holds the answer. What it is for a physical system to be conscious is for it to have a large amount of integrated information (Phi) in it (Tononi et al. 2016). This view, which can be taken to be offering a high-level physical account of consciousness, has some extremely counter-intuitive consequences. For example, as noted by Scott Aaronson (2014), it predicts that if a simple 2-D grid has ten times the amount of integrated information as my brain, the grid is ten times more conscious! What exactly is meant by one system being more conscious than another has also not been made fully clear by advocates of the theory, but for present purposes, it suffices to note that what it is for an amount of integrated information to be large is patently vague and thus the view is of no help to those who want to hold that consciousness is sharp and broadly physical.

A response to this difficulty is to say that *some* degree of consciousness goes along with *any* amount greater than zero of integrated information. So, consciousness is sharp, after all. This requires us to agree that thermostats are conscious as are speedometers, since they contain some integrated information, and that seems a line to be avoided, if at all possible! But even if you disagree here, as noted above, there remains the question as to what it is for one system to have a greater amount of consciousness than another. And since advocates of integrated information theory accept that certain 2-D grids are more conscious than human brains, it cannot have to do with the number of experiences or the intensity of the experiences; for surely no one wants to hold that the relevant grids have more experiences or more intense experiences than our brains (Pautz 2019). What is meant by saying that they are more conscious then?

An alternative strategy is to accept, for the reasons given, that consciousness is not to be reduced to properties found in the physical sciences or to functional properties having inputs and outputs built up from such physical properties or informational properties but to insist that consciousness is broadly physical nonetheless, since it is metaphysically *grounded* in lower-level physical properties. This needs a little explanation. Following Fine (2012), to say that a property P is metaphysically grounded in a property Q is to say (a) that it is metaphysically necessary that whenever Q is instantiated, P is too, and (b) that the nature of P explains why P is metaphysically necessitated by Q. As an illustration, consider the disjunctive property of being red or square. That is metaphysically grounded in the property of being red. It is so since it is metaphysically necessary that whenever the property of being red is instantiated the property of being red or square is instantiated and the nature of the latter property explains why this relationship of necessitation obtains.

The point to be made now is that if consciousness is held to be grounded in lower-level physical properties then there are two possibilities. The first is that the relevant lower-level properties are vague in which case yet again consciousness will be vague; for how could a sharp property have a nature that explains its being metaphysically necessitated by a vague property? Sharp properties are sharp *by* their nature. They are *necessarily* sharp. So, the nature of a sharp property P has no room for vagueness within it and thus that nature cannot *explain* the presence of P in every possible world in which the preferred vague property is present.

Perhaps it will be replied that this is too fast. However puzzling it may initially seem, we can actually give *examples* of sharp properties that are metaphysically grounded in vague ones. Consider the property being colored. That is metaphysically grounded in the property of being red. But being red is vague whilst being colored is sharp.

It is not clear that the property of being colored really is sharp. But let us put that to one side. This case of metaphysical grounding is unproblematic because the property of being colored is just the second-order property of having *a* color and it is a priori that red is a color. So, it is a priori and necessary that anything that is red is colored. But nothing like this obtains in the consciousness case; for suppose that consciousness is metaphysically grounded in vague physical property P. Then, on the model of being colored and being red, there will have to be some second-order physical property of having Q such that consciousness is one and the same as having Q, where having Q is sharp, and P has the property Q and further it is a priori that P has Q. But there is no suitable *sharp* candidate for the (broadly) physical property of having Q. Furthermore, it is a crucial feature of the physicalist metaphysical grounding proposal for consciousness that consciousness not be *reducible* to some broadly physical property. And this is being denied with the claim that consciousness is one and the same as the second-order physical property of having Q.

The conclusion to which we are driven is that consciousness cannot be a sharp property that is metaphysically grounded on vague lower-level physical or functional properties. This brings us to the second possibility with respect to the metaphysical grounding of consciousness, namely that the relevant lower-level properties are complex configurations of *sharp* microphysical properties[3], in which case there will be a really huge number of grounding laws linking consciousness to the microphysical realm. But even if it is supposed that complex configurations of sharp microphysical properties metaphysically necessitate consciousness, no account has been offered (or even seems possible) of how the nature of consciousness *explains* why it is so necessitated. Consider one such case. Call the relevant configuration 'C'. Now consider a minimally different configuration, C* that doesn't metaphysically necessitate consciousness. Microphysically, C and C* are almost the same. Yet C necessitates consciousness and C* doesn't. If

---

[3] On the issue of sharpness in the microphysical realm, see note 4 below.

consciousness itself does not have a physical/functional nature, it is a total mystery as to why C does the job but C* doesn't.

Of course, it could now be held that the grounding is brute. But leaving aside the issue of whether the relation is appropriately called "grounding", the suggestion that consciousness is brutely grounded in the physical is very unsatisfying. Indeed, it puts the physicalist about consciousness in the uncomfortable position of replacing the dualist's brute psycho-physical laws of nature (about which more later) with a host of special, inexplicable, metaphysically necessary pseudo-laws. That surely is to be avoided, if possible.

There is one final way in which premise (2) might be put under pressure. Perhaps consciousness is a physical property that is not to be found in the physical sciences nor is metaphysically grounded in any such property. If this is the case, the possibility opens up that consciousness is a sharp, physical property after all. On the face of it, the suggestion that consciousness might be physical and yet not lie within the physical sciences nor be grounded (only) upon properties referred to therein is incoherent. But there is a view— Russellian Monism—under which it makes good sense. Since Russellian Monism is a complex view which deserves extended discussion, I put it aside for now. I shall return to it in Chapter 2. For the present, I simply note that there is good reason to deny that Russellian Monism, in either of its two standard forms, ultimately can be used to overturn premise (2).

I turn next to premise (3). Consider the origin of the universe and the emergence of more and more complex properties. Take water, for example. Water emerged once hydrogen and oxygen atoms combined in a certain way. Further, there is an explanation as to why they combined in the way they do to form water. Oxygen needs two more electrons to become stable. If oxygen atoms were to go to two hydrogen atoms and take away two electrons from them (one from each), the result would be an O_2 oxide ion and two H^+ ions. These ions are not fully stable. So, instead oxygen atoms share electrons with hydrogen atoms by forming two O-H bonds. The result is H_2O, which is fully stable.

What about properties like being a mountain or being a river? Again, these properties seem reducible to fundamental physical and topic neutral properties arranged in the right ways. So, there is no special or inexplicable emergence in these cases.[4] The case of consciousness is radically different if

---

[4] It might be supposed that there is a puzzle even here, if it is accepted that these macro-properties are themselves vague. But the puzzle arises only on the assumption that reality at the level of microphysics is sharp. This assumption is highly contentious, however. The simplest

consciousness is a sharp, nonphysical property that emerged out of certain brain structures. Here there is no reducibility and relatedly no explanation as to why it emerged as it did. So, uniformity in nature is lost. Phenomena gradually get more and more complex and then suddenly out of the blue something radically different just occurs. Why? There is no explanation. It is just a brute fact that once certain *vague* physical structures are in place, something *sharp* and nonphysical emerges. But that is very difficult to accept or even comprehend. The worry here is related to the one J.J.C. Smart was expressing in the following passage which gives his reaction to the dualist view that there are fundamental phenomenal-physical laws:

> I cannot believe that ultimate laws of nature could relate simple constituents to configurations consisting of perhaps billions of neurons (and goodness knows how many billion billions of ultimate particles) all put together for all the world as though their main purpose in life was to be a negative feedback mechanism of a complicated sort. Such ultimate laws would be like nothing so far known in science. They have a queer "smell" to them. I am just unable to believe in the nomological danglers themselves, or in the laws whereby they would dangle. (1959, p. 143)

The term "nomological dangler" that Smart uses in this passage is due to Feigl (in an essay not itself published until later, as a short book, in 1967). My concern about consciousness is similar to that of Smart's. The idea that consciousness just suddenly emerges without any explanation from certain neural configurations, themselves wholly without consciousness, is puzzling indeed. One wants to ask: why did *this* nonphysical phenomenon just suddenly appear out of the blue, given *these* physical states? Why wouldn't *other* prior physical states have done just as well? But if the laws connecting consciousness to certain physical states are fundamental, then these seemingly sensible questions are illegitimate. And that makes the view that consciousness is a nonphysical phenomenon "frankly unbelievable".

There is also a further dimension to the worry. It is not just that consciousness is nonphysical and tied by a brute law to the physical realm that is difficult to accept. It is also that consciousness is sharp whereas the relevant

---

interpretation of quantum mechanics has it that micro-reality is vague or fuzzy, that properties of micro-entities lacking theoretical values in quantum mechanics are vague properties. Examples would include energy, spin, polarization, and spatio-temporal location. For more here, see Chibeni 2006.

underlying physical states are vague. Why should vague states generate a sharp one?[5] If anything cries out for an explanation, this does. But none is forthcoming—or even possible—if consciousness is nonphysical and so linked only by a brute law to the physical domain.

So, premise (3) seems very plausible. And once premise (3) is accepted along with (2), the first intermediate conclusion of the paradox is established: consciousness is not sharp.

1.2 The Paradox Explained: Part B

However, if consciousness is not sharp, it is vague and, in being vague, it permits borderline cases. Are there any? Here is a possible case. Suppose I have only just woken up, and I am still groggy, I am not yet fully conscious. Isn't this a borderline case of consciousness?

It is certainly a fact that I am *more* conscious of the world around me when I am fully awake than when I first groggily open my eyes. *What* I experience is initially indefinite and impoverished. As I become fully awake, *what* I experience gets richer and richer. But this doesn't show that experience or consciousness itself has borderline cases. Here is how Papineau puts the point:

> If the line between conscious and non-conscious states is not sharp, shouldn't we expect to find borderline cases in our own experience? Yet when we look into ourselves we seem to find a clear line. Pains, tickles, visual experiences and so on are conscious, while the processes which allow us to attach names to faces, or to resolve random dot stereograms are not. True, there are 'half-conscious' experiences, such as the first moments of waking.... But, on reflection, even these special experiences seem to qualify unequivocally as conscious, in the sense that they are like something, rather than nothing.   (1993, p. 125)

Try to think of other clearcut, objectively borderline cases of consciousness, that is, cases such that it is objectively indeterminate whether consciousness is present. Obviously, with some simpler creatures, we may not *know* whether they are conscious. But that is not germane to the issue. You can

---

[5] For more here, see pp. 9–10 earlier.

certainly think of a case of consciousness which is indeterminate as to whether it is a case of pain, say. Think of sensations at the dentist as your teeth are being drilled. Some of these sensations seem impossible to classify as to their species. There is a feeling of pressure perhaps. Is it pain? Not clearly so, but not clearly not. Here it is indeterminate as to what you are feeling, but not indeterminate as to whether you are feeling.

Alternatively, imagine that you are in a hospital bed feeling pain and that you can adjust a dial that controls the delivery of morphine to your body. As you do so, your pain becomes less intense, gradually transforming itself into a feeling of pleasure. In the middle of this process, there may well be experiences that are not easy to classify. Again, there is indeterminacy at such times as to what you are feeling, but there is no indeterminacy as to whether feeling continues to be present.

Consider the case of auditory sensations. Suppose you are participating in an experiment, listening to random high-pitched sounds through headphones. You are asked to press a button for each sound you hear. In some cases, you are unsure whether you are hearing any sound at all. Isn't this a borderline case of consciousness?

We can agree that there is epistemic indeterminacy here: you do not know whether you are hearing any sound. Still, this isn't enough for there to be a borderline case of consciousness. After all, you are listening attentively for a sound; are you hearing a sound or not? Well, even if you aren't hearing a sound, you are still hearing something, namely silence. That is, you are hearing the absence of a sound; it is not that you are failing to hear at all! There is something it is like for you subjectively to hear silence. So, either way, you are hearing and thus experiencing something. So, this doesn't show that there can be borderline cases of experience.

Suppose someone held that being tall is precise, admitting of no borderline cases. We can quickly show this person that she is wrong by presenting her with examples of people who aren't definitely tall but who also aren't definitely not tall. We can do the same with experiencing red or feeling pain or hearing a loud noise or feeling happy. But can we do it with being an experience (or being conscious)?

I don't think we can. We can certainly agree that as the intensity of an experience diminishes, it becomes less and less definite and rich in its character, but either an experience is still there or it isn't. Picturing what it is like from the subject's point of view, we picture the experience gradually changing in its phenomenology until it is so 'washed out' and minimal that it has hardly any distinguishing features subjectively. But the subject is still having an experience. The gradual transition is in the number and intensity of the subjective features of the experience, not in the state's being an experience (being phenomenally conscious).

The model that tempts us here is that of a light bulb with a dimmer switch. As one falls asleep, the light becomes dimmer and dimmer and then suddenly all light is gone. By contrast, as one comes out of anaesthesia, a very faint light suddenly dawns and then it becomes bright. But of course if this is the case, then consciousness is sharp.

Life is not like this. The reason is straightforward: the concept *living* is a functional/behavioral, cluster concept. Living things use energy, they grow, they reproduce, they respond to their environment, they adapt, and they self-regulate. What it is for an entity to be living is for it to have enough of these functional and behavioral features. Borderline cases arise with respect to whether a given entity genuinely does have enough of the relevant features (perhaps it does by my standards but not by yours) and also with respect to the possession of individual features, as, for example, with bacteria and certain kinds of organic molecules. The result is that the transition in the case of life from clearly inanimate to clearly animate beings is gradual and continuous.

In the case of consciousness, there is no functional or behavioral definition. This is why it is perfectly coherent to imagine a creature that is not conscious (a zombie) even though it is functionally and behaviorally just like a creature that is.[6] As noted earlier, the concept of a conscious state is just the concept of an experience, that is, a state such that there is something it is like to undergo it. So, there is nothing in the concept of consciousness that supports the view that there are intermediate stages, as is true for life.

Perhaps it will now be replied that the fact that we cannot give any clear examples of borderline cases of consciousness and the further fact that the concept *consciousness* is not like the concept *life* does not demonstrate that the concept *consciousness* is sharp. Imagine, for example, that we lived in a world with only red objects and only blue objects. In such a world, we might not be able to conceive of a borderline case of red and so we might take it for granted that red is a sharp property (and the concept *red* a sharp concept) and likewise for blue. But we would be wrong. It is metaphysically possible for there to be borderline case of red even if we are not able to conceive of a borderline red thing.

---

[6] This over-simplifies minimally. For more here, see Chapter 2, pp. 7–8.

This seems to me correct as far as it goes. But the issue is what it is reasonable to believe on the basis of evidence rather than what is provable. Conceivability is defeasible evidence for metaphysical possibility and inconceivability is defeasible evidence for metaphysical impossibility. In the latter case, the question is whether what we know by a priori rational reflection upon the relevant concept, given that we possess the concept and a good understanding of it,[7] is good grounds for ruling out the truth of the proposition that it is metaphysically possible that there is an object satisfying the concept. In the case of the concept *tall*, we can easily conceive of a borderline case whether or not we have encountered any borderline tall men. That is evidence for the view that the concept is vague. In the case of the concept *red and green all over* we cannot conceive of an object that satisfies it. Since we possess the constituent concepts here and we have a good grasp of them, that is evidence that it is metaphysically impossible that there is such an object. The concept *consciousness* is such that we cannot conceive of a borderline case and that is prima facie evidence that it is sharp. And what goes for the concept *consciousness* goes for the property of being conscious too.

One reaction to these observations is to say that it is indeed true that our *current* concept of consciousness is sharp but that doesn't mean that it will remain sharp in the future. This is a possibility suggested by Michael Antony in his 2006.[8] He says:

> One can, however, distinguish between our current concept *conscious state* and some future version of the concept, claiming that while our current concept is indeed sharp, a future development of it will be vague. This occurred with the concept *life*. At earlier stages in its history the concept was sharp: borderline living creatures were inconceivable. However, the concept developed with the advent of modern biology, and it now appears to be vague (viruses, for example, are often plausibly suggested as borderline cases). Similarly, it might be thought that our current, relatively primitive concept *conscious state* must undergo developmental change before it can correctly represent its subject matter, one such change being from sharpness

---

[7] Rats cannot conceive of the truth of various true theoretical, scientific propositions but this is no reason to suppose that these propositions are not really (possibly) true. This is because rats lack the relevant concepts. Similarly, if I possess a given concept but I misunderstand it (as in the case of Burge's individual who possesses the concept *fortnight* but thinks that a fortnight is ten days), the fact that I cannot conceive of P's being the case via my a priori reflection on the concept is not grounds for holding that it is metaphysically impossible that P is true.

[8] I should add that Antony does not end up endorsing this suggestion.

to vagueness. In this way, one can admit that our current concept is sharp in accordance with our intuitions, but maintain that the concept is also in a sense vague since a future, more correct version of it will be vague.

(2006, p. 517)

It is not fully clear that the concept *life* really has changed from sharp to vague, as Antony supposes in this passage. Vitalists held that life is a vital, immaterial force animating living things. But this was a view about life itself, not about the concept *life*. There is no inconsistency in holding both that what it is for any organism to be alive is for it to have enough of a certain cluster of functional and behavioral features and that in actual fact what is responsible for any organism's having such a cluster of features is its having a vital, immaterial force within it. The force might be held to be what *realizes* that complex of features.

Still, it must be admitted that vitalists seem to have taken their view to offer an account of the nature of life rather than just a realization of it. From the modern perspective, their concept of life is like the concept *phlogiston* in being an empty natural kind concept. The cluster of features we now take to define life is merely contingently associated with life, on the vitalist view.

This is pretty obviously not a plausible model for understanding how our concept *consciousness* might develop into a vague concept from its current sharp form. For one thing, the idea that it could turn out that consciousness, that is, experience or feeling, never existed, seems prima facie absurd (unlike the idea that there never was any vital force). To consciously think such an idea is to have a conscious experience of thinking and thereby already to refute it! For another thing, any future vague functionalist or behavioral definition would not be a definition of the phenomenon we currently call 'consciousness'; for our current concept has no functionalist or behavioral definition. Since trivially it is a priori *necessary* that our current concept of consciousness is without any such definition, our current concept cannot *develop into* a future vague functionalist or behavioral concept. At best, it could be replaced by such a concept (as was the case with the vitalist's concept of life on the second understanding of it above and our current concept of life). But were such a replacement to occur, it would be a concept for something other than consciousness and therefore the possibility of such a replacement offers no support to the view that consciousness itself might turn out to be vague.

There is a further point worth making here about the above suggestion, namely that it frames the issue in the wrong way. The question of central interest is the question as to whether consciousness itself admits of possible borderline cases. This is not directly a question about concepts at all. So, whether our current concept of consciousness might change through time is really not to the point. What we want to know is whether consciousness is the sort of thing that can have borderline cases. And the conclusion to which we are driven by the reflections of this section is that it is not. Consciousness is not vague. So, consciousness, it seems, is both vague and not vague. What to do? Houston, we have a problem!

2

Russellian Monism to the Rescue?

Russellian Monism (RM) gets its name from a view Bertrand Russell held in 1927 and that he himself called 'neutral monism'. Russell wrote in *The Analysis of Matter* (p. 264):

> . . . we know nothing of the intrinsic quality of the physical world, . . . we know the laws of the physical world, in so far as these are mathematical, pretty well, but we know nothing else about it.

The key preliminary idea is that physical science itself tells us only about the relational/structural properties of matter, including spatiotemporal properties and causal/behavioral dispositions (second-order properties). Physical science leaves open the nature of the categorical bases for these properties—the nature, that is, of the intrinsic properties that occupy the causal/dispositional roles associated with the basic theoretical terms of microphysics.

Here is an illustration. Suppose electrons are basic. Electrons are particles having mass and negative charge. But what are mass and charge? The Russellian monist takes it that these properties are to be cashed out in terms of how electrons behave and interact with other elements of reality. Things having mass attract other things with mass and resist acceleration. What it is for an electron to have mass is for it to have *an* intrinsic property that enables it to behave as just specified (to play the mass role). Electrons have negative charge. Negative charged things attract positively charged things and repel other negatively charged things. What it is for an electron to have negative charge is for it to have *an* intrinsic property that enables it to behave in these ways (to play the negative charge role). Of course, these specifications are very rough and ready. The full story about these roles is told by physics via fundamental physical laws. Generalizing, the properties that physics attributes to elementary particles are structural (that is, pertaining to their arrangement and combinations), causal (nomic), and spatio-temporal. Physics thus has nothing to say about the intrinsic or categorical properties of electrons and likewise for other fundamental particles; or so the Russellian monist holds.

The intrinsic natures of the micro-parts of reality are made up of (presumably a small number of) intrinsic properties called "quiddities". This brings us to a second part of the Russellian Monist view. The fact that we are conscious beings, undergoing a variety of macro-conscious states, is to be understood in terms of there being, among the quiddities, some that we may call "phenomenal quiddities".[1] Consciousness, for the Russellian monist, is *quiddity-involving*. This makes consciousness very different from the rest of (or at any rate a very high percentage of) properties found in the manifest world. Those properties generally are quiddity-neutral. Being a river, being a tree, being a mountain, being made of wood are structural properties in the sense that what matters to their instantiation is how micro-particles are combined into larger structures. Whether the relevant micro-particles (or other fundamental physical particulars) have the same or different quiddities matters not at all. So long as the basic parts of a tree are duplicated structurally at the level of microphysics, chemistry, and the other physical sciences, another tree will result that is a copy of the first one. Whether the same quiddities are present in both cases makes no difference. After all, quiddities are completely undetectable by human beings whatever instruments they use.

Consciousness is different. Whether I feel a pain or an itch depends upon which quiddities are instantiated in me at a micro-level. Only some quiddities ground consciousness and the quiddities relevant to pain are different from those relevant to feeling an itch. So, macro-conscious states are not states that can be realized by different quiddities. There is one cluster of quiddities for pain, another for feeling an itch, and so on. The former quiddities cannot realize the itch feeling and the latter quiddities cannot realize pain (see the simple model in the box below).

Russellian monists now have two options: either they hold that the quiddities crucial to consciousness (the ones I earlier called "phenomenal quiddities") are themselves genuinely experiential properties or they hold more neutrally that there are specific quiddities that *ground* all macro-phenomenal facts. Russellian monists sometimes call the latter quiddities "proto-phenomenal properties".

---

[1] Amy Kind (forthcoming) notes that if it is allowed that there are multiple kinds of quiddity, then the view isn't really a *monistic* view at all. Better to call it "Russellian pluralism". I agree with Kind that the usage of the term 'monism' isn't happy.

Scenario 1

P1 has quiddities, Q and S
P2 has quiddities, Q and W
P1 bears arrangement relation R to P2
P1 and P2 are fundamental micro-particulars

Scenario 2

P1 has quiddities, Q and W
P2 has quiddities, Q and S
P1 bears arrangement relation R to P2
P1 and P2 are fundamental micro-particulars

According to the Russellian monist, scenario 2 contains a different physical complex from scenario 1, but there is no structural difference between the two. So long as the difference is *only* at the level of quiddities, two scenarios cannot differ with respect to the presence of a tree (or a rock or a river). If one contains a tree (or a rock or a river), so does the other. But if two scenarios that are structurally identical differ at the level of quiddities, one can contain a pain and the other an itch (or no feeling at all). Difference in the relevant quiddities is what makes a crucial difference with respect to the tokening of macro-phenomenal properties.

The former of these two views is sometimes also called "panpsychism", though panpsychists often hold more strongly that *everything* in the universe, no matter how large or how small, is conscious, and that is no part of the Russellian monist position (as I am understanding it). But why should we believe that among the quiddities are some that are *phenomenal* in character? Why hold that there are very primitive forms of consciousness found even at the level of microphysical reality?

One possible answer is this: humans undergo complex conscious states, ranging from emotions and moods to sensory experiences and bodily feelings. We all agree that animals less sophisticated than us undergo conscious states, even though those states are not as wide ranging as ours. Think about pigs or dogs or chickens. And there is good reason to think that consciousness extends even into the realm of insects (Tye 2016). One possibility is that as organisms get simpler and simpler, there is a sharp cut-off point, and experience, whatever its stripe, ceases. But another possibility is that it continues in simpler and simpler forms, that the light of consciousness fades but never fully goes out, being found even in inorganic matter, indeed being found at the level of the most basic entities in matter (for example, quarks and electrons).

The trouble with this answer is that it allows consciousness to be present in structures, large and small, whether or not a brain is present. It is now hard to see how the Russellian monist can *avoid* the extreme panpsychist view that absolutely everything is conscious, including rocks and trees and thermometers.

A better answer, it seems to me, is for the Russellian monist to say that the usual physicalist accounts of consciousness all fail (as is shown by a myriad of familiar arguments) and they do so because consciousness itself is irreducible or at least has irreducible components. Our consciousness, and that of other animals as different as honeybees and pigs, arise from the right combinations of these irreducible components (the phenomenal quiddities) and those combinations are not found in all complex systems, including rocks and trees and thermometers.

As noted above, Russellian monists who hold that the quiddities possessed by the most basic microphysical entities are only proto-phenomenal take a less extreme stance, holding only that some of the quiddities, combined in the right ways, *generate* consciousness. They thus can easily allow that many entities, small and large, including quarks, electrons, and rocks, all lack consciousness.

Russellian Monism (RM), in its standard presentation, has a third aspect to it: the view is a form of a priori physicalism. Thus, Russellian monists accept that a super-intelligent being could deduce a priori all the macro-conscious facts, given knowledge of all the phenomenally relevant quiddities and how they are combined (their pattern of instantiation) in creatures' brains.

We might argue about whether RM is really a physicalist view. One thing at least is clear: RM differs from the usual forms of physicalism in its reliance on quiddities and its assertion that specific quiddities are crucial to macro-conscious states. Still, the quiddities postulated in RM are found in things that are unconscious as well as in things that are conscious—in trees and rocks, for example. They occur across all of nature at the most fundamental level. Further, their possessors obey fundamental physical laws. So, why not count RM as a physicalist view?

Of course, if the Russellian monist holds that some quiddities are genuinely phenomenal properties, then some physical things will have subjective properties as well as objective ones. And this might lead some to deny that RM is really a form of physicalism. Still, this seems to me a verbal dispute about how to use the term 'physicalism' and for present purposes I am happy to allow that admitting phenomenal micro-quiddities does not preclude classifying the view as physical.

Russellian monists can say that they agree with dualists about the conceivability of zombies. Zombies are conceivable, they can claim, since it is conceivable that there are beings the same as us except for the phenomenally relevant quiddities. These beings are structurally, functionally, and behaviorally just like us but they lack any conscious states.

Alternatively, Russellian monists can say that zombies are not *fully* conceivable since beings that are full physical duplicates of us will have to be physical duplicates not just at the level of structural or dynamic properties but also intrinsically. This is the line Chalmers takes in his 2002, p. 266:

> Some . . . monists may hold that a complete physical description must be expanded to include an intrinsic description, *and may consequently deny that zombies are conceivable.* (We think we are conceiving of a physically identical system only because we overlook intrinsic properties.)

On this view, what are really conceivable are *structural* zombies. Torin Alter and Dirk Pereboom (2019) concur. They comment:

> Regarding the conceivability argument, Russellian physicalists can argue as follows. On reflection, a zombie world is not ideally conceivable. If such a world initially appears conceivable, this is because we mistake a zombie world for a *structural* zombie world: a consciousness-free world that (minimally) duplicates all of the actual world's structural features. If there is an ideally conceivable world in the vicinity, then that world is a structural zombie world. There is no good reason to accept the ideal conceivability of a full-fledged zombie world, which would lack consciousness despite duplicating not only the actual world's structural features but its quiddistic features as well.

Whichever line on zombies is preferred, Russellian monists can agree with dualists that there is a strong link between conceivability and metaphysical possibility that is not defeated here. So, RM can be held to combine virtues of both physicalism and dualism. It allows for the metaphysical possibility of structural zombies while still embracing a physicalist worldview. It also avoids the brute phenomenal-physical laws posited by the dualist. These considerations make up what Chalmers calls "the Hegelian synthesis argument for Russellian Monism".

2.1 Versions of Russellian Monism

There are two versions of RM, as it is usually presented. The reductive version is held by, for example, Grover Maxwell (1978), Dan Stoljar (2001 and 2006), David Chalmers (1995 and 1997 (less strongly in his 2012)), and Barbara Montero (2010). This version of RM is an identity thesis. As a way of introducing the view, let us say that a phenomenal state type is a type of state with a *felt* character to it. Examples would be the feeling of intense pain, the visual experience of red, the feeling of anger, the feeling of an itch. These states are all conscious states: each one has a distinctive 'feel' to it. For each state, there is something it is like to be in it. The most general phenomenal state type is simply that of being an experience. Consciousness itself, as it is of interest in this book and as explained earlier in the elaboration of the paradox in Chapter 1, just is experience.

Reductive RM is *not* the thesis that macro-phenomenal types are each identical with types of the following sort: having micro-parts with so-and-so phenomenal quiddities, $Q_1, Q_2, .. Q_n$. This does not explain why humans are conscious and pieces of wood are not; for the micro-parts of humans are the same as the micro-parts of pieces of wood, if physicalism is true. So, the micro-quiddities of our micro-parts are also to be found in the micro-parts of pieces of wood.

The crucial difference is that we have brains and pieces of wood do not. So, the relevant identities must be of the following form:

Macro-phenomenal state type T (for example, the feeling of pain) is identical with having micro-parts with phenomenal quiddities, $Q_1, Q_2, .. Q_n$, arranged to form a certain brain state type N (or functional type of a sort supported by brains).

Primitivist RM takes the following form:

Macro-phenomenal state type T (for example, the feeling of pain) is metaphysically grounded in having micro-parts with proto-phenomenal quiddities, Q_1, Q_2,..Q_n, arranged to form a certain brain state type N (or functional type of a sort supported by brains).

Metaphysical grounding does not require identity. The fact that P or Q is true is metaphysically grounded in the fact that P is true or the fact that Q is true, but there is here no identity. As noted in Chapter 1, metaphysical grounding requires metaphysical necessitation and explanation. The fact that P is true or the fact that Q is true metaphysically necessitates the fact that P or Q is true. Further, the nature of the disjunctive fact that P or Q explains why it is metaphysically necessitated by the fact that P or the fact that Q.

The question we must now ask is whether RM, in either of the above forms, really can help with our paradox of consciousness. To answer this question, let us look first at the reductive version of RM.

2.2 Objections to Reductive Russellian Monism

A consequence of reductive RM is that the physical types with which macro-phenomenal states are to be identified are vague, since neurophysiological types are vague, and likewise for the relevant functional types. So, conscious-ness itself (being the most general macro-phenomenal type: experience) now turns out to be vague and RM is of no assistance with the paradox.

Here is a second problem. RM, as noted earlier, is motivated in part by considerations of conceivability. Recall Chalmer's Hegelian Synthesis Argument for the view. Structural zombies are conceivable, and therefore metaphysically possible; but this is compatible with physicalism because a structural zombie duplicate of me is not a duplicate of me at the level of quiddities. In my structural zombie duplicate, my phenomenal quiddities are replaced by non-phenomenal ones that play the same structural roles. So, if reductive RM is correct, structural zombies are indeed metaphysically possible just as we pre-theoretically suppose, given their conceivability.

The problem this creates has to do with other conceivable scenarios. It seems conceivable that a stone momentarily feels pain. It also seems con-ceivable that something that has no parts does, something mereologically simple. Let us suppose that souls are mereologically simple, as Descartes held. Then, on the face of it, it is conceivable that souls feel pain. So, given the accepted link between conceivability and metaphysical possibility, it is met-aphysically possible that souls feel pain. But pain, according to reductive RM, is one and the same as having so-and-so phenomenally relevant quiddities arranged to form brain state B (or functional state F of a sort supported by brains). So, it is metaphysically necessary that pain is found only where brain state B (or functional state F) is found. With a soul, however, there is no brain state B. Indeed there are no parts at all and so it is also hard to see how functional state F could be supported.[2] So, the very considerations that motivate reductive RM end up presenting a problem for the view.

There is a further difficulty for reductive RM, related to the difficulty broached above for the case of the putative quiddity of consciousness. Macro-phenomenal states vary dramatically—the feeling of elation, the experience of an itch, the feeling of anger, the experience of bright red. The idea that it could be deduced which macro-conscious states are present at various times in various creatures, using as premises *only* information about quiddities (themselves not involving such states) plus facts about how those quiddities are arranged in the creatures' brains seems a wild leap of faith. Why should we believe it? After all, the quiddities generally are very different from macro-phenomenal states; for it would be absurd to hold that quarks feel pains and itches and experience colors. So how could the presence of so-and-so macro-phenomenal states be deduced a priori from the presence of such-and-such quiddities together with brain state information? There is surely a strong temptation to ask: why should *these* quiddities give rise to *that* macro-phenomenal state rather than *this* one? The explanatory gap this question rests on is reminiscent of the one that has been held to arise for standard physicalist views.

The worry is captured well in the following passage from Chalmers (1995):

> On the face of it, our conscious experience does not seem to be any sort of sum of microphenomenal properties corresponding to the fundamental physical features in our brain, for example. Our experience seems much more holistic than that, and much more homogeneous than any simple sum would be... If the roots of phenomenology are exhausted by micro-phenomenology, then it is hard to see how smooth, structured macroscopic phenomenology could be derived: we might expect some sort of 'jagged,' unstructured phenomenal collection instead.   (p. 306)

---

[2] Adam Pautz raises essentially this objection in his forthcoming. One might question whether it really is true to say that the relevant functional state could not be supported by a soul, given a suitably narrow and counterfactual characterization of that state (as the state (very crudely) that would be caused in the soul by bodily damage were the soul normally embodied and that would cause avoidance behavior in such a situation, etc).

This worry dates back to Wilfrid Sellars and his discussion in the 1960s of the visual experience of a pink ice-cube. How, wondered Sellars (1963), does phenomenal pinkness arise? What accounts for its homogeneity in our experience? It certainly doesn't *seem* to be composed of anything more simple.

There is, then, a *combination* problem for the Russellian monist about macro-phenomenal states.[3] If these states are simple, then there is real emergence and reductive Russellian Monism is false. On the other hand, if macro-phenomenal states are generated from combinations of micro-phenomenal states, then why is it that they seem (in some cases at any rate) so simple, so utterly lacking in components?

You might reply that there would be no explanatory gap for a super-intelligent being even if there is for us, as we raise the question. But the phenomenal quiddities are agreed to be very different from macro-phenomenal states such as the feeling of pain, so why should we suppose that the explanatory gap disappears even for such a being? If the explanatory gap stays open, then it is conceivable that the quiddities are present in whatever configurations are deemed relevant and the macro-phenomenal states are arranged differently. And if this is the case, then there is no a priori deducibility and RM is no longer a version of a priori physicalism.

There is a further dimension to the combination problem for reductive Russellian Monism. If various experience types are tokened at the micro-level, then it seems that there should be psychological subjects of experiences at that level, micro-subjects.[4] What is the relationship of these micro-subjects to ordinary people who are the subjects of macro-phenomenology? Some philosophers say that the tiny subjects combine or merge or fuse to form the macro-subjects (Seager forthcoming).[5] But how is this achieved? It is very difficult to see how a satisfactory answer can be given to this question on the basis of a priori reflection.

Perhaps it will now be suggested that the aprioricity of reductive RM needs to be repudiated. This is the line taken by Pat Lewtas (2013, 2017). Lewtas suggests that there is a 'mental chemistry' that "takes micro-experiences as raw material and refashions them into a single unified micro-experience". He claims that this process necessarily decreases the number of subjects and

---

[3] For criticisms of panpsychism in connection with the combination problem, see Goff 2006, 2009; also Coleman 2014.

[4] I return to this issue in detail in Chapter 4.

[5] This is denied by Luke Roelofs. Roelofs is a universalist. On his view, everything, no matter how complex or simple, is conscious, including rocks and Ned Block's China-Body system. Moreover, simple subjects do not fuse or merge to form single macroscopic subjects. This highly counter-intuitive view, which is no part of RM in its standard form, is defended by Roelofs in his 2019.

compares it to what goes on when two streams of consciousness of a split brain subject merge into one stream at the end of a typical split brain psychological experiment.

The model of split brain subjects appealed to here is highly controversial. I have argued elsewhere that claiming that there are two different split brain subjects undergoing disconnected experiences during the experiment (2003) is misguided. But even leaving this to one side, the idea that there is a mental chemistry, the full principles of which are not discoverable by a priori reflection not only undermines some of the motivation for RM but also leaves the view with having to say that macroscopic phenomenal properties are *hidden* combinations of microscopic phenomenal properties. Not only are the combinations hidden here but so too are the microscopic phenomenal properties. Somehow these all mix so as to present us with the phenomenology with which we are familiar, the phenomenal pinkness as we view Sellars' ice-cube, the phenomenal sweetness as we suck on a cube of sugar, and so on. This leaves the view with very little advantage over the regular type B identity theory. Let me explain.

Type B identity theory is an a posteriori view. It holds that pain, for example, is one and the same as so-and-so brain state but that this identity cannot be discovered by a priori reflection. The mental chemistry version of reductive RM holds that pain is one and the same as such-and-such quiddities arranged in such-and-such ways (via the principles of 'mental chemistry') to form so-and-so brain state even though again no amount of a priori reflection will show this to be true. Likewise for all other macro-conscious states. What advantage is reductive RM now supposed to have over type B identity theory? Reductive RM now effectively accepts that pain is one and the same as a certain brain state. All it adds is that the brain state itself is built out of certain hidden combinations of hidden quiddities. The latter is supposedly an a posteriori claim but it is unsupported by any scientific investigation. In this respect, the view is actually worse off than type B identity theory!

The conclusion to which we are driven, it seems to me, is that reductive RM is a highly problematic view that does not provide any clear rescue at all with respect to the paradox. Does primitivist RM fare any better?

2.3 Objections to Primitivist Russellian Monism

As noted earlier, primitivist RM rejects the identity claim of reductive RM and holds instead a grounding thesis for macro-phenomenal types.

This view might seem to allow a physicalist response to the paradox as follows. The macro-phenomenal type *consciousness* is itself sharp and metaphysically grounded in a type of the form: having micro-parts with *proto-phenomenal* quiddities, Q_1, Q_2,..Q_n, arranged to form a certain brain state type N (or functional type F).

The trouble is that it is radically unclear how the above complex, vague, and partly neurological (or functional) type could metaphysically ground the sharp type *consciousness*. After all, metaphysical grounding is supposed to have an explanatory dimension. But on the face of it there is again a huge explanatory gap here. There is nothing, it seems, in the nature of the sharp type *consciousness* that explains why it is metaphysically necessitated by the micro-quiddities combining to form brain state N (or functional type F for that matter).

Relatedly, on one standard view of metaphysical grounding (that of Fine), metaphysical grounding derives from essence. It is of the essence of the conjunctive fact that P and Q that it be grounded in the fact that P and the fact that Q. But anyone who holds that consciousness is sharp and distinct from any underlying physical properties will likely also endorse the thesis of revelation with respect to consciousness, according to which consciousness has *no* hidden essence. This is because once consciousness is held to be distinct from the quiddities, there doesn't seem to be anything left which could constitute the hidden essence of consciousness. Furthermore, if consciousness has a *hidden* essence then how can the presence of consciousness be deduced a priori from information about micro-quiddities (not themselves involving consciousness) and the physical combinations of their micro-parts in brains? It seems that primitivist RM eats its own tail, as it were. We are told that a great virtue of RM is that it takes intuitions about conceivability *seriously*, but then it transpires that, on the primitivist version of the view, conceivability has to go by the wayside.

The upshot is that it is not at all clear how this view has any advantage over regular type B physicalism; nor does there seem any reason to prefer the view to dualism even though its advocates often write as if it avoids the complexities of dualism. In place of the basic, brute, contingent, phenomenal-physical laws of the dualist connecting conscious states with the physical, there are now basic, brute, metaphysically necessary laws connecting the same. These grounding laws are special and quite unlike any other laws. This is so because they are metaphysically necessary instead of being nomically necessary, as other laws are, and they go across levels, bridging physical facts about arrangements of proto-phenomenal quiddities and phenomenal facts. The disunity introduced here is hard to motivate as is the additional complexity unless it can be shown that every other alternative that avoids such an extreme disunity is simply untenable. That, as I shall argue in the next two chapters, is not the case.

One strategy the Russellian monist might now adopt is to propose that the metaphysical grounding of consciousness on quiddities is to be understood on the model of the grounding of determinable qualities on determinate ones. Consider, for example, the color red. Something's being red is metaphysically grounded on its being a determinate shade of red, red_{27}, say, since it is metaphysically necessary that things that are red_{27} are red and it is in the very nature of the determinate/determinable relationship that something's having a determinable quality is metaphysically necessitated by its having a determinate of that determinable. On this picture of metaphysical grounding, it is not the essence of the grounded property that is crucial to the grounding (as on the account of grounding adopted thus far, following Fine) but rather the essence of the determinable/determinate relationship. In the case of consciousness, then, the thought is that consciousness is a determinable quality having as its determinates properties of the type: having microparts with quiddities, Q_1, Q_2,..Q_n, arranged to form a certain brain state type N (or functional type F).

On the face of it, this proposal gets things backwards; for consciousness must be taken to be sharp, it seems, if the paradox is to be avoided, but the determinate physical properties (either neural or functional) that metaphysically ground consciousness are all vague. In the case of red and red_{27}, it is the other way around. The color red is vague; red_{27} is sharp. So, how can the case of the grounding of determinable qualities by determinate ones be used to shed light on the grounding of consciousness on quiddities?[6]

A possible reply is to say that in other cases of determinates and determinables, the determinable is sharp but at least some determinates are vague. Here I have in mind the earlier example of being colored (sharp, arguably) and being red (vague). Unfortunately, this example is not applicable for the reasons given in Chapter 1.[7]

I conclude that primitivist RM is no more helpful than reductive RM in dealing with the paradox. Indeed, all things considered, it does even worse!

---

[6] This point, independent of Russellian Monism, also creates trouble for those (for example, Stephen Yablo (1992)) who hold that the relationship of the phenomenal to the physical is to be modelled on that of the relationship of determinable qualities to determinate ones.

[7] See here Chapter 1, pp. 10–11.

2.4 A Final Concern

One more general issue for RM is worth briefly mentioning in conclusion. As noted earlier, part of the motivation of RM, in its standard form, is to preserve the link between conceivability and metaphysical possibility and thus to allow that zombies are metaphysically possible. Consider, then, the behavior in me that is caused by my being in some given phenomenal state P. My structural zombie duplicate will behave as I do even though at the micro-level, the quiddities in him are not phenomenally relevant and thus P is missing. Given this, what causal difference does the presence of *phenomenally* relevant quiddities in me make to my behavior? Even if those phenomenally relevant quiddities are absent, so long as there is duplication at the level of processes posited by the physical sciences, as is the case for my structural zombie duplicate, the very same behavior results.

It is well known that neurophysiology casts a shadow over standard forms of dualism. The additional nonphysical properties posited by the dualist seem to make no difference to behavior since the same behavior would have resulted as actually results from some given phenomenal state even if that state had been missing, so long as the neurophysiological processes remain constant (as the dualist allows is metaphysically possible). On the face of it, the same kind of worry arises for RM notwithstanding the fact that it is not a dualist view.

I shall return to this issue in Chapter 4. Whatever one's reaction here,[8] the overall conclusion I draw from the discussion of the present chapter is that RM, as it is usually elaborated, is beset by objections to which there are no clear answers and thus is a dead end as far as the paradox goes. What, then, is the solution to the paradox? In the next chapter, by way of preparation for my answer to this question, I turn to the representationalist view of consciousness and a remark made by G.E. Moore about consciousness and transparency.

---

[8] My own reaction to this particular worry is that it can be answered by the Russellian monist, given the distinctions and framework proposed in the final section of Chapter 4.

3

Transparency and Representationalism

In this chapter, I want to take another look at the phenomenon of transparency and the thesis of representationalism. As will become clear, there are several different versions of representationalism. It is important for my overall position that I clarify which version I still embrace.[1]

3.1 The Transparency Thesis

I begin with four quotations, two from G.E. Moore, one from Gilbert Harman, and one from an earlier essay of mine:

> ...that which makes the sensation of blue a mental fact seems to escape us; it seems, if I may use a metaphor, to be transparent—we look through it and see nothing but the blue... (Moore 1903, p. 446)

> When we try to introspect the sensation of blue, all we can see is the blue: the other element is as if it were diaphanous. (Moore 1903, p. 450)

> When Eloise sees a tree before her, the colors she experiences are all experienced as features of the tree and its surroundings. None of them are experienced as intrinsic features of her experience. Nor does she experience any features of anything as intrinsic features of her experiences. And that is true of you too...Look at a tree and try to turn your attention to intrinsic features of your visual experience. I predict that you will find that the only features there to turn your attention to will be features of the tree... (Harman 1990, p. 667)

> Standing on the beach in Santa Barbara a couple of summers ago on a bright sunny day, I found myself transfixed by the intense blue of the Pacific Ocean. Was I not here delighting in the phenomenal aspects of my

---

[1] Parts of this chapter draw on several earlier essays of mine, most notably Tye 2008, Tye 2014, and Tye 2017.

visual experience? And if I was, doesn't this show that there are visual qualia? I am not convinced. It seems to me that what I found so pleasing in the above instance, what I was focusing on, as it were, were a certain shade and intensity of the colour blue.... When one tries to focus on [the sensation of blue] in introspection one cannot help but see right through it so that what one actually ends up attending to is the real colour blue.

(Tye 1992, p. 160)

Generalizing from the above passages and extrapolating away from Harman's restriction to intrinsic features, the key transparency claims are as follows: in a case of normal visual perception, if we introspect:

1) We are not aware of features of our visual experience.
2) We are not aware of the visual experience itself.
3) We cannot attend to features of the visual experience.
4) The only features of which we are aware and to which we can attend are external features (colors and shapes of surfaces, for example).

(1), (2), and (4) are to be understood as claims about de re awareness. There is nowhere in these claims or in the quoted passages any mention of *direct* awareness. As far as awareness goes, the thesis is that when we try to introspect a visual experience occurring in normal perception, we are not aware of the experience or its features (intrinsic or not) *period*. This, I take it, is the basic thesis of transparency, as it applies to visual experience. The basic thesis is naturally extended to cases of illusory perception and hallucination. In the case of illusion, claims (1), (2), and (3) are unchanged. (4) becomes

(4') The only features of which we are aware and to which we can attend are features experienced as (or presented as) belonging to the external particulars.

In the case of hallucinations, (4), in my view, should be replaced by

(4") The only features of which we are aware and to which we can attend are locally un-instantiated features of a sort that, if they belong to anything, belong to external particulars.

I ignore here cases of veridical hallucinations. I also concede that (4") is contentious; for it requires the admission that we can be aware of (and indeed attend to) un-instantiated properties. I shall return to this later. For the moment, let us restrict ourselves to cases of normal visual perception and let us take the thesis of transparency to be directed to the experiences that occur then.

3.2 Qualia Realism

Qualia realism is the thesis that experiences have intrinsic features that are non-intentional and of which we can be directly aware via introspection. Such features are commonly known as *qualia*. According to the qualia realist, the phenomenal character of an experience (what it is like subjectively to undergo the experience) is one and the same as the cluster of such intrinsic features. This thesis is often coupled with the further thesis that perceptual experiences have intentional features (as Block (1990) and Shoemaker (1994) hold) but the latter claim is not a necessary part of qualia realism. Adverbialism, for example, is a form of qualia realism but, according to (standard) adverbialism, experiences do not have intentional features. I shall say something about qualia realism and the sense-datum theory later.

Qualia realism is inconsistent with transparency. So, those who accept transparency see it as providing an argument against qualia realism. Dan Stoljar demurs. He comments:

> If those who use transparency to argue against qualia realism appeal to the thesis that ... one is not aware in introspection of one's experience, then it would be fair to say that it should be treated as presenting a paradox rather than as something to which one might look to decide between competing positions in philosophy of mind. For surely it is a datum, something on which everybody can agree, that one can be aware of one's experience in introspection! (Stoljar 2004)

I disagree. The datum on which everyone should agree is that if I am having a sensation of blue then via introspection I can be aware *that* I am having such a sensation. This is fact-awareness, not de re awareness of. I can be aware of the fact that *p*, aware *that p*, without being aware *of* either the particulars or the properties that comprise the fact that *p* or that make it a fact that *p*, as Fred Dretske (1999) has emphasized. For example, sitting in the kitchen, if I hear the timer ding then I am aware that the muffins in the oven are cooked. But (facing the other direction) I am not aware of the muffins, nor the oven, nor for that matter the property of being cooked. I am aware rather of the timer (before me in plain view) and of the property of dinging.[2] Furthermore, to suppose that it is a *datum* that when I introspect, I am aware (de re) *of* my visual experience of blue is to rule out, from the get-go, the view that having a visual experience is not a matter of standing in a relation to a mental particular but rather a matter of my instantiating the property of experiencing blue, where this view is committed to the existence of me and the property but not to such an entity as my instantiating the property of experiencing blue at the relevant time. It seems to me that we shouldn't close off that metaphysical option a priori.

It is also worth noting that ordinary talk of my being aware of my experience when I introspect is neutral on the question of whether such awareness is de re. Compare:

(5) I am aware of my penchant for driving fast.

There is a natural non-de re reading of this, namely,

(5a) I am aware that I have a penchant for driving fast.

Of course, I am not denying that there may be a de re reading too. Here is another example

(6) I am aware of your interest in fine wines.

(6) has a natural de dicto reading as

(6a) I am aware that you are interested in fine wines.

3.3 Two Arguments from Transparency Against Qualia Realism

The first argument, based on awareness, is very simple. It proceeds as follows:

---

[2] I can be aware of a concrete particular in some cases by being aware of a part of that particular. So, there is such a thing as indirect de re awareness; but it evidently is not applicable here to the case of the muffins.

(7) Experiences have intrinsic features that are non-intentional and of which we can be directly aware via introspection (qualia realism).

The features alluded to in (7) make up the phenomenal character of the experience.

(8) In normal perception, we cannot be aware of features of our experiences via introspection (transparency).[3]

So,

(9) Qualia realism is false.

The second argument, based on attention, is more complicated. One claim that might be made by the qualia realist in opposition to those who try to wield transparency against their view is that although we can't *perceptually* or *sensorily* attend to our visual experiences or their qualities, still we can *cognitively* attend to them. The obvious question to ask of those who hold this view is "What is cognitive attention?" According to Stoljar (2004), a person cognitively attends to something just in case she thinks about that thing. For example, according to Stoljar, if I tell you that we will next attend to the second flaw in the argument, this is merely a matter of our thinking next about that flaw. Now, since, of course, we can think about our experiences and their properties—we can debate their nature, wonder how they fit into the natural world, etc—it follows that we can attend to them.

This account of cognitive attention is a little simple-minded. A better proposal is that cognitive attention is a matter of thinking about something *in a focused way*. If one is thinking about something in the course of idly day-dreaming about a variety of matters, one isn't really attending to that thing. This is a consequence, it seems plausible to suppose, of the ordinary concept of attention. Here let me draw on the views of Alan R. White (1964).

According to White, the concept *attending* is a polymorphous concept:

[T]here are many different activities, the doing of which can in certain circumstances count as attending and yet none of which in other circumstances necessarily counts as attending. Another example of a

---

[3] In my view, in no case of perception can we be aware of such features by introspection.

polymorphous concept is the concept *working*. One can work by running or talking or sitting, but equally one can do each of these things without working.

To say that someone is attending, White claims, gives us no more idea as to what specific activities he is engaged in than to say he is working. To describe someone as attending, on this view, is to say that there is *some* specific activity the person is engaged in that is focused on something that occupies her (where that same activity in another context when not focused on the relevant thing does not constitute attending to it). For example, one can attend to an argument by reading it but one can read an argument without attending to it. In the cognitive case, the activity is thinking.[4]

Suppose, then, that the argument from transparency, based on attention, against qualia realism is stated as follows:

(10) We cannot attend to the qualities of our visual experiences.

Therefore,

(11) Qualia realism is false.

If the argument goes this way, the qualia realist can simply reply that the premise is false; for we can cognitively attend to the qualities of our experiences. We can think about them in a focused way. Alternatively, if 'attend' in (10) means *sensorily attend*, then the premise is true, the qualia realist may say, but the argument is invalid.

It seems to me that this appeal to two sorts of attention misses the point. If one is aware (de re) of some entity, one's awareness directly puts one in a position/enables one to form de re cognitive attitudes with respect to that entity. After all, if one cannot even ask "What's that?" with respect to some entity directly on the basis of one's awareness, surely one isn't aware *of* that entity. Think about the case of distorting glass, for example. One can see something moving on the other side but one hasn't a clue what it is. The glass distorts its shape too much. Still, in seeing the thing, one is aware of it

---

[4] These remarks about attention are intended to be consonant with how we ordinarily think of attention. But prima facie they do not fit very well with some scientific discussions of attention. In particular, they seem not to capture what scientists sometimes call 'diffuse' or 'ambient' attention (Pashler 1998).

and in being aware of it, one can at least ask "What's that?" with respect to the thing.[5]

Here is a further example. Suppose a moth on a tree trunk is *perfectly* camouflaged. Is one then aware/conscious of it? Intuitively no. But why not? Because one's awareness does not put one directly in a position even to ask "What is that?" with respect to it.

Now forming a de re cognitive attitude with respect to a thing directly on the basis of one's awareness requires attending to that thing at least in normal circumstances.[6] So, if one cannot attend to a thing in such circumstances, then one is not aware of that thing. This leads to the following version of the argument from transparency, based on attention, against qualia realism:

(12) If one is aware of one's visual experience or any of its qualities when one introspects, then in normal cases one *can* attend to one or more of those items directly on the basis of that awareness.

(13) But one cannot so attend.

So,

(14) One is not aware *of* one's visual experience and/or its qualities when

one introspects in normal cases.

So,

(15) Qualia realism is false.

This is my preferred version of the transparency argument based on attention in the case of visual experience.

---

[5] This test for awareness, as stated, oversimplifies minimally. Suppose, for example, you put your head around the door of my office and ask me if I'd like to go to lunch. I see your head. Do I also see you? Intuitively I do. Cases like this can be handled either by modifying the test so that the demonstrative is permitted to pick out some sufficiently large or salient part of the relevant thing or by arguing that the demonstrative can be applied directly to the thing even though only part of it is in the field of view.

[6] My own view is that this is the case in all circumstances. For a defense of this stronger claim against putative counter-examples, see Tye 2010. For present purposes, the stronger claim is not needed.

3.4 How Does Transparency Support Representationalism for Visual Experience?

So, transparency creates trouble for qualia realism. But how does it support representationalism? If, as I believe, the transparency thesis can be extended to cases of abnormal perception, then it follows that the qualities of which one is aware when one tries to introspect a visual experience are not qualities of the experience. What, then, are they? A plausible hypothesis is that they are qualities *represented* by the experience. Since these are the only qualities of which one is (and can be) aware, a further plausible hypothesis is that necessarily (visual) experiences that are alike with respect to the qualities they represent are alike phenomenally. This is the most basic thesis of representationalism.[7]

Now property representationalism is not the only form of representationalism. A more common form is content representationalism (Tye 1995). Content representationalism, in my present view, is not supported by the phenomenon of transparency. What I want to do next is to say a few things about content representationalism and the question of how it is best elucidated and why, in my view, it encounters difficulty where property representationalism does not.

One way to try to motivate content representationalism is by appeal to introspectable difference between experiences. This is the line Jeff Speaks takes in his 2009. He argues in this way:

(16) If there is an introspectable difference between two experiences, then there is a difference in the objects and properties those two experiences represent as in one's environment. (Transparency/Difference Principle)

(17) If there is a difference in the objects and properties two experiences represent as in one's environment, there is a difference in the content of the two experiences.

(18) Conclusion. If two experiences differ in phenomenal character, they differ in content.

---

[7] There's a complication here I'm ignoring for moment. More on this later. I should also add that some representationalists (myself included) want to extend this thesis not only to all perceptual experiences but also to all experiences *period*.

My immediate reaction to Speaks' argument is that (16), as stated, is puzzling. When is there a difference in objects and properties, as understood in (16)? Presumably just in case there is a difference in objects and/or properties. But where there is an introspectable difference and a difference in objects, there will be a difference in properties. So, all that really matters is the difference in properties.

Also (17) is problematic. Speaks argues convincingly that Fregean content won't do, given transparency. And the Fregean line conflicts anyway with the very plausible view that the content of experience is (at least partly) nonconceptual. However, Russellian singular content gets into trouble with hallucinations and the need there for gappy content, as I have argued at length elsewhere (Sainsbury and Tye 2011). One solution is to opt for existential content, but this also seems to me unsatisfactory. If I see a particular tomato (call it 'Tom'), the content of my experience isn't just that there is *something* before me that is red and round and bulgy; for Tom intuitively is crucial to the accuracy of my actual experience. After all, it is *Tom* that looks red, round, and bulgy to me. Had Tom not been present, my actual experience would not have matched the world.

The obvious remaining alternative as far as content goes is the view that the content is a set of possible worlds. In the case of Tom, the relevant set is the set of worlds at which Tom is red, round, and bulgy. What if Tom had not existed and I, the subject of the experience, had introduced 'Tom' as a name for what I erroneously took myself to be seeing? Now 'Tom' is an empty rigid designator. So, the set of possible worlds at which Tom is red, round, and bulgy is the empty set. In both the veridical case and the hallucinatory cases, then, there is a content (though not the same one) and the accuracy conditions in the veridical case involve a real, external particular (as they should).

On this view, (18) is false. To see this, consider two phenomenally different hallucinatory experiences. They differ in the properties they represent (given transparency) but not in their content (for each, the content is the empty set). This not only undermines the above argument for content representationalism but also creates direct trouble for the thesis itself. According to the content representationalist, on both the strong and weak variants, experiences that are alike in their content are alike in their phenomenal character. But phenomenally different hallucinatory experiences have the same content. The conclusion I draw is that if we are going to be representationalists, we should be property representationalists (Tye 2017).

3.5 Blur

Many cases have been adduced as counter-examples to the view that necessarily visual experiences that are alike with respect to what they represent are alike phenomenally. I have responded to a large range of these counter-examples previously (Tye 2003, Tye 2006a). One case that keeps coming up in the literature is that of blur. In opposition to my critics, I hold that blur is not in the least problematic for the transparency thesis. This section is devoted to explaining why.

Here is Tim Crane on blurriness as a problem for representationalism:

> I remove my glasses and things seem blurry. Introspecting this experience, blurriness does certainly seem to be instantiated somewhere. But does it seem to be instantiated in the familiar objects of experience? ... When I say that 'everything seems blurry' I don't mean that it seems as if the things around me are blurry ... What I mean is that I am experiencing things in a blurry way. Isn't this a straightforward case of where one can be 'directly' aware of an aspect of one's experience which is not an aspect of the objects of experience?   (2006, p. 130)

A.O. Smith concurs:

> There is a feature that objects themselves can appear to have that bears some similarity to blurriness: what I shall call 'fuzziness'. A cloud, or an Impressionistic water-colour figure, or a patch of light projected on to a screen, can have an indistinct boundary and can hence look fuzzy. This, however, is quite different from blur. Fuzziness, unlike blur, is and is taken to be a feature of the object seen ... Blurriness is not a way that things in the world themselves seem to be. It is, however, a feature of experience of which we are usually aware when it is there. The Transparency Thesis is therefore false.   (2008, p. 201)

I agree with Crane and Smith that seeing an object, X, blurrily is not the same as seeing X as itself fuzzy, nor is it the same as X's looking fuzzy. In the latter two cases, if X is sharp, there is misrepresentation. Fuzziness is in the content. Seeing X blurrily is a matter of X's causing (in the right way) a visual experience that represents X's surface boundaries indistinctly. This is out of focus or blurry vision. A visual experience represents X's spatial boundaries indistinctly so long as the visual experience represents X's boundaries but does *not* represent exactly where they lie. Blurriness, thus, is not a feature of the object seen but neither is it a feature of the experience. Not having feature F is not a feature of a thing; so neither is having G *and* not having F.

Thus, I also agree with *some* of what Janet Levin says in the following passage (2019, p. 254):

> ... [blurriness and distortion] do not seem to be diaphanous; in turning our attention to further features of... blurry or distorted visual experiences, we don't seem to be directing our attention to the objects these experiences represent.

I agree that when I introspect a blurry experience of an object O, I am indeed not turning my attention to blurriness as a feature of O. But equally I am not turning my attention to blurriness as a feature of my experience. To repeat: blurriness is not a property (feature) of objects (though fuzziness is in some cases); nor is blurriness a property (feature) of experiences. A so-called 'blurry experience' is really an experience that represents boundaries of objects indistinctly. When I introspect such an experience, I am simply aware *that* I am seeing blurrily.

When an object X looks fuzzy to me, my experience represents X as having boundaries and also represents that there is no determinate fact as to exactly where they lie. If X is fuzzy, for example, as with a water color that has run or a cloud, my experience is accurate. When X looks sharp, my experience represents X as having boundaries and it represents exactly where they lie. When I experience X through a blur, my experience represents X as having boundaries somewhere in a certain region around X, but it does not represent exactly where in that region the boundaries are.

Could I be in a position such that I couldn't tell whether I am seeing, for example, a sharp word, through a blur or whether the word itself is fuzzy and I am seeing it clearly? Yes. In some cases, one cannot tell from one's experience whether the thing one is seeing is fuzzy or sharp. One can't see it clearly enough to decide. In such a case, one's experience doesn't represent either. When this happens, one is seeing blurrily.

Consider the example in Figure 1. Here one is actually seeing a word with vague boundaries on the fourth line from the top, as one knows full well, given the surrounding words (and the sharpness of other text), but one cannot tell that from the character of one's experience of that word *alone*

Figure 1.

and so one is seeing the word blurrily. In such a case, one's experience represents the boundaries of the letters indistinctly. The word, taken on its own without information supplied by the background context, does not *look* to be sharp nor does it *look* to be fuzzy. One's experience, given the restriction just noted, does not represent whether the word has sharp boundaries or fuzzy ones. It leaves that open. One is simply seeing the word through a blur.

Blurriness, then, is consistent with the thesis of transparency with respect to visual experience. There is nothing in the phenomenon of blurriness that threatens the representationalist view of visual experience.

3.6 Extending Transparency: Bodily Sensations

So far I have discussed transparency in connection with visual experiences. But my representationalism extends to other sorts of experiences. Consider first non-visual perceptual experiences. Auditory experiences represent sounds. If I introspect an experience of a loud noise on my left, what I am aware *of* is the property of being a loud noise on my left, a property that I experience as being instantiated: it sounds to me as if a loud noise is on my left. Olfactory experiences represent smells; gustatory experiences represent tastes; tactual experiences represent textures. In each of these cases, there are various properties of which I am aware when I introspect—for example, being smell S (that of rotten eggs, say), being sweet, being smooth and in contact with my left thumb, and so on. To repeat: this awareness is purely de re. It is not awareness-that or awareness-as. In each case, as I undergo the given sort of experience, I am aware of a certain property without being aware of its internal nature if it has one; indeed, I need not be aware of *any* facts about the property, nor am I required to conceptualize it in any way in order to be aware of it. By being aware of the relevant properties, I am aware that I am experiencing such-and-such an auditory experience, olfactory experience, gustatory experience, or tactual experience. The properties experienced need not be instantiated in my local environment, of course. I might be suffering an illusion or hallucinating. Indeed, it is consistent with representationalism that *nothing* really has the relevant properties, that there really are no loud noises or rotten egg smells, etc. The point is that these properties are *experienced* as instantiated and that it is my awareness *of* them that grounds my introspective awareness *that* I am undergoing so-and-so experiences. Moreover, as with visual experiences, if you tell me to focus my attention on the experience itself, I find that my attention slips through my experience to what I am experiencing. The experiences themselves, thus, are transparent to me.

Bodily sensations are to be handled similarly. Take the case of pain. You can't feel pain without being in pain and you can't be in pain without feeling pain. Why? The obvious answer is that pain itself is a feeling. Being in pain and feeling pain are one and the same. For pain, *esse est percipi*.

If pain is a feeling, then pains are naturally taken to be token feelings. On this view, a pain in a leg is not a token feeling located inside the leg but rather a token of the leg pain (pain in a leg) feeling. For such a pain, there are two components to the feeling: there's the locational component and there's the painfulness of the feeling. The locational component can be shared with feelings that are not painful. A tickle in a leg, for example, is also a feeling. What makes a feeling an 'in a leg' feeling? Not that the feeling is in a leg obviously. Nor that a disturbance is going on in a leg; for, as noted above, one can feel a pain (tickle) in a leg even if one lacks a leg. A plausible answer is that a feeling is an 'in a leg' feeling just in case it is a feeling that *represents* that a disturbance or state or condition of some sort or other is to be found in a leg. Since misrepresentation is possible, there is now no difficulty in understanding how there can be a phantom leg feeling, be it a pain, a tickle, an itch, or whatever (Armstrong 1962).

This proposal is naturally cashed out further by saying that it is the character and location of the disturbance that determines the phenomenology of the feeling. A pain in a leg represents a leg disturbance of one sort; a tickle in a leg represents a leg disturbance of another sort; and so on.

Suppose that you have a pain in a leg. You are told to pay attention to your pain. Where does your attention go? To the disturbance you feel to be occurring in your leg and its qualities. Those qualities, or at least some of those qualities are ones that you dislike strongly. The disturbance itself is not a pain for reasons already given. Let me quickly add another. Suppose that you have a referred pain. You feel a pain in your left arm, but the disturbance you experience is actually in your heart. The case is one of misrepresentation. If the disturbance in your heart were a pain, then you would feel a pain in your heart. But you don't. You feel a pain in your arm.[8]

Pain, on the representational view, is Mother Nature's way of telling Her creatures that they have damaged, or are in the process of damaging, their bodies. Pain is like the red warning light on the dashboard of your car that flashes when the oil level is too low (Byrne 2012). The system has been designed so that the light (pain) is difficult to ignore. You may ignore it, of course, but the message is that you ignore it at your peril.

Pains (I hold) represent tissue damage just as the flashing red warning light represents critically low oil.[9] Pains, of course, vary in how they feel; and this seems tied in part to variations in qualities of the represented tissue damage (notably, its shape, volume and intensity, and its location).[10] A stabbing pain represents tissue damage with a well-defined and bounded volume and a distinctive dagger-like shape occurring in a precise location; an ache represents tissue damage or irritation with a much vaguer shape and volume and (relatedly) a much less precise location.

Let me say a little more about phantom limb pain. This phenomenon is summarized below by Nikolajsen and Jensen (2001).

The first medical description of post-amputation sensation was given by Ambroise Paré (1510–1590), a French military surgeon, who noticed that patients may complain of severe pain in the missing limb following amputation.... In modern times, traumatic amputations originating from World War I and II, Vietnam and Israeli wars and from landmine

---

[8] This answers Block who asks whether if the disturbance is in your heart, the pain is in your heart. See his 2006. The *disturbance* of which you are conscious is in your heart but your experience 'places' it in your arm. The case is like that of experiencing someone as being straight ahead when in reality she is off to the right, a mirror having been placed in front of you at forty five degrees. Of course, the disturbance of which you are conscious need not have the very non-locational properties you experience it as having any more than the person on the right need have all the non-locational properties you experience her as having. Perhaps, the mirror is slightly distorting, for example.

[9] One difference is that you, the driver of the car, are aware of the warning light. But if transparency holds, you, the subject of the pain experience, are not conscious of the pain. Rather you are conscious of what the pain represents.

[10] Pains may also represent whether the tissue damage is thermally, mechanically, or chemically produced. There is also a question as to whether the represented tissue damage has to be actual. It is certainly the case that pain is sometimes felt when the skin is under sharp pressure without having yet broken as when one walks on a very sharply edged rock in bare feet. Here the tissue damage is impending.

explosions all over the world are a tragic cause of phantom pain in otherwise healthy people. Other major reasons for amputation and phantom pain are peripheral vascular disease and neoplasms. Today, it is common knowledge that virtually all amputees experience phantom sensations, painful or not, after limb amputation. Non-painful phantom sensations rarely pose a clinical problem. However, in some amputees, the phantom becomes the site of severe pain, which may be exceedingly difficult to treat.   (p. 107)

In phantom pain (or phantom limb pain), one feels a pain in a limb that no longer exists. As noted above, this is nicely accounted for by the representational view: the subject is hallucinating. He or she has an experience that represents a disturbance in a limb and there is no such disturbance (nor any limb).

It is sometimes objected that you cannot really *have* a pain in your left leg if your left leg has been amputated. But you can *feel* a pain there. You can have a 'pain in your left leg' feeling, with or without a left leg. So, a distinction needs to be drawn between pain and the feeling of pain; and such a distinction is not available on the representational view.

It seems to me, however, that the temptation to say that you cannot really have a pain in your left leg if you lack a left leg extends equally to the claim that you cannot really feel a pain in your left leg without such a leg. It has nothing to do with any distinction between having a pain and feeling a pain. Rather it derives from the use of a definite description within an intensional context. To illustrate: suppose you and I are listing creatures in Austin we fear. You say that you fear my cat. I say that I fear the dog next door. You then point out to me that actually there is no dog next door. Given this context, we can agree that I don't *really* fear the dog next door, for there is no such dog to fear. Here effectively we give the description 'the dog next door' wide scope and so we interpret the claim that I fear the dog next door as saying that the dog next door is such that I fear it. So, given that there is no dog next door, the claim is false.

Suppose, however, you and I are listing phobias. Among other things, I tell you that I fear the dog next door. My fear here is real even if there is no such dog. Given this context, it is true that I fear the dog next door. This is possible because the definite description is now taking narrow scope relative to the psychological verb.

Corresponding remarks apply to the case of your feeling a pain in your left leg. If you assert that you feel such a pain, I may reply, "Don't be silly!

You no longer have a left leg." In so replying, I am taking the expression 'my left leg' in your report, 'I feel a pain in my left leg,' to have wide scope. But I may also agree with your remark, knowing full well that you appreciate that your left leg is missing. Given this background presupposition, I am giving 'my left leg' narrow scope.

What goes for feeling a pain in your left leg goes for having a pain in your left leg. When you complain of having severe pain in your left leg, I need not correct you. I can take your report to be expressing a truth, just as in the case of feeling a pain in your left leg.

So far, I have suggested that pains represent tissue damage (and also that they may represent whether the damage is thermally, mechanically, or chemically produced). Unfortunately, if that is all that pains represent then it becomes very difficult to understand one salient aspect of their phenomenal character, namely their "negative affect". Pains don't merely inform us of the presence of some disturbance at a location in our bodies; they *hurt*. A theory that says that pain experiences merely represent tissue damage at some location in one's body would seem to leave out the painfulness of pain.

Likewise, a theory that says that the feeling of orgasm only represents certain physical changes in the region of the genitals doesn't begin to explain the highly positive affect of orgasms. What needs to be added? Well, the obvious explanation of the popularity of orgasms is that they *feel* good and the obvious explanation for why people and other sentient creatures do their best to avoid pain is that pains *feel* bad. Feeling good and feeling bad are plausibly viewed as representational features of experiences. More specifically, my suggestion, in the case of pain, is that pains not only represent physical and locational properties of tissue damage, but (in first approximation) they also represent the valuational property of being bad.

That valuational properties are represented in experience is supported by some recent work by Palmer and Schloss (2010) on color experience. Presented with a colored square on a monitor screen, when subjects are asked to rate how much they like the color, it was found that they tend to prefer blue, red, and green and they show least preference for dark yellow and brown. These preferences are based on how the colors *look* to the subjects. Some colors just look better than others. What does this involve? My proposal: some colors are represented as better or more pleasing to us than others. It is interesting to note, incidentally, that blue is the color of clear skies and clean water, red the color of ripe fruit, and green the color of fresh vegetation whereas dark yellow is the color of vomit and rotten food, and brown the color of biological waste. Perhaps these facts play a role in accounting historically for why some colors look better to us than others.

These remarks are consistent with transparency. When we introspect our experiences, be they bodily or perceptual, we come across a wide array of qualities. Among the qualities of which we are then aware are valuational qualities. Some colors look pleasing to us; some bodily disturbances feel bad. That this is the case is manifest to us when we introspect our experiences. By being aware of such qualities, we are aware *that* we are undergoing pleasant or unpleasant experiences of one sort or another.

3.7 Emotions and Moods

The emotions on which I shall focus in this section are what are sometimes called 'primary emotions'. These are emotions that are universally felt, emotions liability to which is inherited. Such emotions are usually divided into the following types: anger, fear, happiness, sadness, and disgust.

According to William James (1884, 1890), emotions are perceptions of bodily changes. He comments:

> If we fancy some strong emotion and then try to abstract from our consciousness of it all the feelings of its bodily symptoms, we find that we have nothing left behind.   (1890)

James continues:

> What kind of emotion of fear would be left if the feeling neither of quickened heart beats nor of shallow breathing, neither of trembling lips nor of weakened limbs, neither of goose flesh nor of visceral stirrings, were present, it is quite impossible for me to think. Can one fancy the state of rage and picture no ebullition in the chest, no flushing of the face, no dilatation of the nostrils, no clenching of the teeth, no impulse to vigorous action, but in their stead limp muscles, calm breathing, and a placid face?
> (1884, p. 193)

There seems much that is right in these remarks. Suppose you suddenly feel *extremely* angry. As you do so, your body changes in the sorts of ways James notes as well as in others (for example, your arteries constrict and your blood

pressure rises, your heart pounds, your voice becomes louder). These physical changes are registered in the sensory receptors distributed throughout
your body. Via the activity in these receptors, you sense the bodily changes
that are taking place. Intuitively, in feeling anger, you are sensing these
changes. James' theory goes beyond this, however. According to James, the
experience of anger *just is* the perception of the relevant bodily changes. And
here there is a difficulty, first raised by William Cannon (1929). For surely,
on at least some occasions, there is very little difference in the bodily
reactions associated with different emotions.

Take the following case, for example. I have what I think is the winning
lottery ticket, as I see the string of winning numbers for the lottery appear on
the television screen before me. In my excitement, I misread the eighth
number in the string; and a moment or two later, as I look at the screen
again, I realize my error. I experience immediate anguish. I am subject to
two different emotional experiences, but my state of bodily arousal immediately after I realize my error is similar to my state before. Alternatively,
suppose I am on a roller coaster ride and I am scared stiff. A day later, I am
experiencing great anger, as I see a man across the street beating a dog with a
baseball bat. My internal bodily states in both cases are very much alike but
again the emotions experienced are different.

The point that different emotional experiences can involve the perception
of similar bodily changes is supported by experiments in psychology, the
most famous of which was performed by Stanley Schacter and Jerome Singer
(1962). In this experiment, subjects were injected with the stimulant, epi-
nephrine. They were then placed in different settings. Some of the subjects
were put in a room with a confederate who acted out anger; others were sent
off to a room with a confederate who played the part of someone euphoric
and amusing. The subjects reported experiencing emotions mimicking those
of the confederate.

These points do not refute James' theory. More recent research (LeDoux
1996) has shown that where different primary emotions are experienced, the
bodily states perceived or felt, although importantly alike at a coarse-grained
level, nonetheless vary along a number of underlying physical dimensions.
Still, there remains a serious objection. Emotional experiences are typically
directed on things in the world outside the body. This is evident not just
from the ways in which we normally describe such experiences but also from
their phenomenology. Perceptions of bodily changes, however, are directed
inwards. It seems, then, that there is more to an emotional experience than
the perception of an appropriate set of bodily changes. Even so, James had

an important insight: for primary emotions at least, the experience of the emotion *partly* involves a feeling or perception of changes in the body.

Emotions, as noted above, are typically directed at things or persons. This is true not only of human emotions but also of those experienced by creatures belonging to other species. A dog with the hair on its neck standing upright, a dog that growls at you and bares its teeth as you walk into its territory, is a dog of which you should be very wary; for such a dog is angry and its anger is directed at you. The dog has detected your presence—it has seen you—and this perception has triggered in the dog a state of bodily arousal which it is feeling.

But why should your presence make the dog angry? After all, if the owner of the dog had been there in your place, the dog would have been subject to a very different emotion. Intuitively, the dog senses the *invasiveness* of your behavior. You have the look of an intruder to the dog. It is via this perception of you that the dog's anger gets to be directed at you.

Here is another example. Suppose you are in a dark parking lot, late at night, walking towards your car. You hear someone (or something) moving behind you. Suddenly you feel very scared. In these circumstances, your body changes both internally and externally. For example, your face goes white, your stomach churns, your heart rate speeds up, your legs go weak. These changes are ones you sense; but why do they occur? What causes them? The obvious answer is: your auditory perception of the person (or thing) behind you. That person (or thing) sounds threatening. You are thereby fearful of whomever (or whatever) it is that sounds that way. Your experience of fear gets to be directed on an entity outside you by means of a sensory experience of that entity, an experience that represents the entity as threatening or dangerous.

One straightforward proposal, then, is that primary emotional experiences acquire their (typical) outward directedness via the corresponding directedness of a perceptual experience. This proposal, in my view, is too simple as it stands and needs further qualifications.[11] But the basic idea seems to me correct. And if this is the case, then there is no *new* problem presented by the case of emotional experiences. What has been said about perceptual and bodily experiences applies mutatis mutandis here. And just as in the case of the latter two sorts of experiences, valuational properties are represented, for example being bad (for the subject), so too in the case of

---

[11] For example, in some cases, conscious thoughts may take the place of perceptual experiences. For more here, see Tye 2008.

emotional experiences.[12] Emotional experiences, thus, are as transparent as perceptual experiences and bodily sensations.

I should add that in saying that emotional experiences involve representations of value, I do not mean *moral* value. In the case of the feeling of disgust at the vomit on the sidewalk, the experience represents the vomit and its odor as having a kind of negative value, as being foul. Patently, this value is not moral. Similarly, the experience of fear represents the feared object as having another kind of negative value, as being threatening or dangerous. For the experience of anger, the relevant value is that of being invasive or injurious. In the case of the experiences of happiness and sadness, the values are very general positive and negative ones, species of which have just been adumbrated for anger, fear, and disgust.

These values, I claim, are represented to us in our basic perceptual experience of the world. Things look red and square; they sound loud; they taste sweet and sour. But they also look dangerous or encroaching; they smell foul; they look good or they taste bad. These evaluative qualities are as directly given to us in our perceptual experiences as are such qualities as colors and shapes.

This may seem strange, especially to those who think of sense experience on the model of the British Empiricists as involving the sensing of sense data. But the proposal I am making fits well with the ways we ordinarily think and speak about experience. In everyday life, we say things like "That feels good; that smells bad; that looks harmful; that sounds threatening". There is, I suggest, no good reason not to take this talk at face value.

Of course, in some cases we come to learn through trial and error that certain things possess positive or negative values. We learn, for example, that certain things are dangerous which did not previously look dangerous. Subsequently, we come to see them *as* dangerous. In so doing, we subsume them under the concept *dangerous*.

Turning now to the case of moods, the biggest problem they present is that they are not usually directed on anything. One can just feel happy or depressed, period. But if there is no directedness, then there is no representation, it may be said, and so moods that differ will be the same representationally (they represent nothing) and thus, if representationalism is true, they will be the same phenomenally. Patently however, they are not. What it is like to feel depressed is radically different from what it is like to feel happy.

---

[12] In Tye 1995, I did not make clear this connection between value and the emotions. But see Tye 2003, chapter 3. See also Seager forthcoming.

It seems to me that one natural reply is that the experience of endogenous elation is directed on the world generally. The subject thinks that the world is a wonderful place (or something similar); the subject also experiences a certain characteristic bodily state (one that the subject wants to continue); and the contents of both the bodily experience and the thought enter into the overall content of the experience of elation. It does not seem to be part of endogenous elation, however, that the subject experience the world as *causing* his or her bodily state. Such a proposal would introduce massive error into the experience of endogenous elation; for the world as a whole patently does not cause the internal changes. In lacking a causal tie in the content, the experience seems different from, say, the elation felt by a young academic who has just heard that she has gotten a paper accepted by a major journal. In this case, it surely does *feel* to the academic that the wonderful news is the source of the glow in her cheeks, the quickening of her step, the smile on her lips, etc.

An alternative way of handling the case of endogenous elation is to say that the source of our inclination to suppose that there is no intentional object in cases such as this derives from the fact that the object that is the focus of the experience varies through time. So, it might be held that, as I experience elation, initially my experience is directed on the blueness of the sky, say; a moment later, my continuing experience of elation is directed on melodious sounds of music; after that, my attention is grabbed by a spider and I experience elation at the wonderful pattern of the spider web; and so on. Perhaps at some moments, my experience is directed on the whole scene before my eyes rather than some particular thing in the scene (or the whole field of sound, for example). On this view, as my experience of elation continues, its object changes. But even though there is no single object, each object is represented in the same way as wonderful.

Both suggestions fit nicely with the following remarks by Robert Benchley (from his essay, entitled "The Tooth, the Whole Tooth, and Nothing but the Tooth") about the general elation felt by one who has just survived his time in the dentist's chair in the 1920s:

> Heigh-ho! Here's the elevator man! A charming fellow! You wonder if he knows that you have just had a tooth filled. You feel tempted to tell him and slap him on the back. You feel tempted to tell everyone in the bright, cheery street. And what a wonderful street it is too! All full of nice, black snow and water. After all, Life is sweet! (1921, p. 83)

Figure 2.

There is another possibility, however. Consider the case of visual experience again. Where there is a seen object, a given visual experience represents it as having the represented properties via the appropriate causal/contextual connection between the experience and the seen object. In the case of hallucination, there are properties represented but no question of accuracy arises, since the relevant causal/contextual relation is missing.

The suggestion, thus, is that visual experiences are, in this respect, like instruments. Consider the fuel gauge in Figure 2.

The fuel gauge itself does not represent any particular gas tank. It simply has marks on it that represent various fuel levels. Once hooked up, as shown here, it represents the fuel level in a particular tank via its causal connection with that tank. And it can do so accurately or inaccurately. Without being hooked up, no question of accuracy arises.[13] Likewise, I suggest, for visual experiences.

It may be wondered whether it is part of commonsense that hallucinatory experiences are inaccurate. I think not. Hallucinatory experiences are *unsuccessful* experiences. They aim to make contact with the world but fail. So, they are not accurate. But equally they are not inaccurate either. They are not candidates for accuracy.

What about veridical hallucinations? What if I hallucinate a blue ball bouncing before me, say, and, as it happens, there is such a ball? This, I suggest, is like the case of the speedometer lying disconnected on the front seat of my car with the pointer momentarily registering '30' (due to the car hitting a large bump and the pointer flipping to that number on the gauge) while the car happens to be going 30 mph. Is my speedometer here fortuitously accurate? No, for it is not connected to my car. And without any connection, why pick this car to evaluate accuracy? Is it inaccurate? No, for the same reason. Still the speed it represents happens to match the speed of my car. Correspondingly, my hallucinatory visual experience is not veridical

---

[13] Can't there be an inaccurate or faulty gauge that is not hooked up? Yes, of course. But in calling such a gauge "inaccurate", all we mean is that if it were hooked up, it would not accurately represent the fuel level of the relevant vehicle.

since it is not accurate (nor is it inaccurate). But the properties it represents happen to match the properties the ball possesses. Generalizing, veridical hallucinations are literally impossible.

The thesis that emerges here has it that visual experiences represent properties and do so essentially (in something like the manner of instruments, though experiences have a representational complexity to them not found in instruments[14]). However, only some, not all, visual experiences have accuracy-evaluable representational contents. Thus, having an accuracy-evaluable content is not essential to a visual experience.

This proposal has a counterpart in the case of mood experiences. Mood experiences are not accurate or inaccurate. There is no accuracy evaluable content. Nonetheless, they represent properties—valuational ones. The experience of happiness represents a positive valuational property (being wonderful, good to a high degree). The experience of depression represents another valuational property (being awful, negative to a high degree). Mood experiences that represent the same properties feel the same. And when we introspect, it is the properties the experiences represent that we come across. Transparency reigns here as it does for other sorts of experiences.[15]

Not everyone agrees. For example, Amy Kind (2013) comments:

> For transparency to be true of moods, it would have to be the case that whenever one tried to focus one's attention on a mood itself, one's attention would slip right through the experience to something else—perhaps worldly objects, or perhaps the state of one's body. But this isn't at all what happens. It might be that in attending to my experience of bluishness, I don't (or even can't) attend directly to the bluishness of my experience itself. But in attending to my experience of elation, it seems most natural to describe what I'm attending to as the elation itself. I'm not simply attending to some feature of the world, or to a feature of a changing series of things, or even to some unbound feature. Rather, I focus directly on what it feels like to be elated.

I agree with Kind that if I am asked to report what I am introspectively aware of while I am feeling elated, I may perhaps reply: "I am aware of being (feeling) elated." But what I mean here is that I am aware of *my* being (feeling)

---

[14] See here Tye 2017 and below.
[15] For example, in some cases, conscious thoughts may take the place of perceptual experiences. For more here, see Tye 2010.

elated. And this is (covert) fact awareness: I am aware *that* I am (feel) elated. In addition to this fact awareness, am I introspectively aware (de re) of my token experience of elation or the property it has of being an instance of elation? It doesn't seem to me that I am. Suppose I take a drug that suddenly makes me feel elated. The drug lasts five minutes, then afterwards I feel depressed for five minutes. What exactly seems to me to change here? Initially, life suddenly seems wonderful: everything is fun, great, fantastic (and that includes me). Later, life seems drab to me: everything is uninterest-ing, pointless, not worth making any effort to engage (and again that includes me). Introspecting, the properties of which I am aware initially are positive valuational properties; later they are negative ones. These properties are not properties of my mental state. My mental state isn't fun, fantastic, drab, pointless. Equally, these properties need not be ones that seem to me, in undergoing the above moods, to attach to some particular things I encounter and not to others. Perhaps there is a general subject—the world or life—but it seems more plausible to hold that all I really experience here, in undergoing the moods, is just the relevant properties. In this way, the properties are free-floating or unbound (to use a term from Mendelovici 2013). Still, they are the properties I find when I introspect. To acknowledge this is not to give up the representational view. On the contrary, it is to realize that properties can be represented even when propositions are not.

Kind dismisses this view. She asks what it could mean to attend to an unbound property. My answer is that the case is like that of the man who hallucinates something red. In so doing, the man can certainly attend to the color red. The fact that there is actually nothing red in the vicinity is irrelevant. The property exists; the man is aware of it and, being aware of it, he can attend to it.[16]

3.8 Conscious Thoughts

As I read the soccer reports in the newspaper, I am struck with the sudden thought that Manchester United will not win the Premier League any time in the next five years. A feeling of depression comes over me. My body stiffens with annoyance. There is something it is like for me as this occurs. The phenomenology is complex, deriving from my mood, my associated bodily

---

[16] For more on the hallucination case, see section 3.10 below.

sensations and the thought itself (and perhaps some images of goals missed or great goals scored in the past). In thinking the above thought, I have an auditory experience of myself uttering *in foro interno* the English sentence, "Manchester United will not win the Premier League in the next five years," and doing so with my usual pattern of stress and intonation. This auditory experience has its own phenomenology and it can be handled representationally in the manner explained earlier for perceptual experiences generally.

Some say that the above account misses out the phenomenology of the thought itself, that the content of the thought introduces some additional phenomenology, not reducible to the phenomenology of associated bodily sensations or my mood or any further images I might have. This I deny. Of course, I do not deny that the thought itself is a conscious one and that it differs from conscious thoughts with different contents. But to say that the thought here is conscious is simply to say that, as I undergo the thought, I am introspectively aware that I am thinking that Manchester United will not win the Premier League any time in the next five years. This is a matter of higher order consciousness—awareness that so-and-so mental state is present, and the state of higher-order consciousness varies with the first-order mental state. This does not require that there be any additional phenomenology associated with the first-order state over and above the complex phenomenology distinguished above. To suppose otherwise, it seems to me, is to have a picture of introspective awareness as an internal scanner lighting up our internal states and revealing how they 'look' to us, so to speak. Thoughts with different contents 'look' different under the light of the internal scanner and thus they have a different phenomenology.

This is a picture that the qualia realist standardly accepts but it seems to me to fundamentally misconceive the nature of introspective awareness. We do not scan our mental states when we introspect as we might scan external objects with our eyes. Were this the case, we would expect introspection to have its own distinctive phenomenology just as seeing does. But there is no phenomenology of introspection. What are we doing when we introspect then? Answer: in the case of experiences, we are attending to external objects (if there are any) and their experienced qualities. By being aware of these things, we are aware *that* we are undergoing experiences of such and such kinds. Introspection, on this view, is like displaced perception (Dretske 1999; Tye 2014), as noted earlier.[17]

---

[17] One important difference is that in standard cases of displaced perception there is a background belief linking what is the subject is aware of and the content of the secondary

One way to get a handle on what is being claimed here is to think of a robot that has been programmed to move around its environment in a war zone, scan objects it encounters, and classify them as dangerous or not. When it encounters an object with a high assessed level of danger, it issues a report of the following form: I am detecting a dangerous object in position P.

This robot has been built to detect external objects. It does so by using its scanner. It has no scanner for its own internal states. It does not detect those inner states triggered by external objects. The robot is built so that when a certain condition is met (it encounters an object with a certain danger level), it issues a report as specified above—assuming it is working as designed.

We are a tiny bit like such a robot. In the case of vision, we scan our environment with our eyes, detecting various objects and classifying them as being of various kinds. In our case, the detection is conscious. We are *aware* of these objects and their qualities. We experience them. Under certain conditions, using our faculty of introspection, we issue reports (to ourselves) of what we are aware *of*. Via introspection, we judge or believe that we are aware of so-and-so. In this way, we are aware *that* we are aware *of* so-and-so. As noted above (on pp. 34–35), this awareness-that is like the kind of awareness I have when I am aware that the muffins are cooked by hearing the timer ding. The latter awareness-that is secondary in that, unlike the fact awareness possessed by someone who is observing the muffins directly (someone with primary awareness that the muffins are cooked), I am not aware of the muffins or their being cooked. Rather I am aware of something else (namely the timer and its dinging). Correspondingly, I am not aware *of* my awareness of so-and-so objects and features when I introspect. I am aware of something else (namely the external objects and their perceived features).

We are built by nature to operate in this way. The faculty of introspection is wired in; and when all is going as it should, it issues in internal reports of the type: I am aware of (experiencing) so-and-so. And this is true not just for the case of our introspective awareness 'of' visual experiences but also for our introspective awareness of experiences generally. In the case of bodily sensations, we scan our bodies and become aware via introspection that we are aware of certain experienced bodily changes. In the case of felt moods and emotions, we are aware of subtle, and sometimes not at all subtle, shifts

awareness-that. In the muffin case, this is the belief that the timer's dinging indicates that the muffins are fully cooked. This is not so (or need not be so) in the case of introspective awareness. See below.

in our bodily states as well as external things and affective qualities of one sort or another. Via introspection, we are then aware *that* we are aware of these items.

This simplifies minimally. If the experiences are hallucinatory, we are still aware of properties, albeit un-instantiated ones, but we are not aware of the relevant objects (for there are no relevant objects at hand). In such a case, the subject can be aware of, for example, the color red, by vision, and also be aware that she is aware of the color red, by introspection.

What about the case of introspecting our own thoughts? Again, there is no scanning of an inner object. Nor need there be any scanning of an external object. What happens rather is that when we undergo first-order thoughts and we utilize our faculty of introspection, we are built to undergo the corresponding second-order thought. If the first-order thought is encoded in a sentence 'P', the second-order thought generated by the use of the faculty of introspection (when all is going well) is encoded in a sentence of the form "I am thinking that P" or its counterpart in another language.

3.9 More on Property Representationalism

The basic thesis of property representationalism is that necessarily experiences that are alike in the properties they represent are alike in their phenomenal character. There is a complication, however.

Prima facie, an experience as of a red square to the left of a green triangle represents the same properties as an experience as of a red triangle to the left of a green square, namely, being red, being square, being triangular, being green, and being to the left of. But the experiences are phenomenally different.

To this I reply that the experiences represent different sensible property complexes and this is what makes them phenomenally different. One represents the property of being an x and the property of being a y such that x is a red square and y is a green triangle and x is to the left of y. Not so the other. So, either we can take property complexes to fall within the general metaphysical category of property in which case the above thesis of property representationalism needs no revision or we can restate the thesis slightly. Following Mark Johnston (2004), let us call the relevant complexes, "sensible profiles". Now the thesis is that necessarily, experiences that represent the same sensible profiles are the same phenomenally.

The general picture here is one in which external properties play the counterpart role to qualia, on the qualia realist's view, and sensible property complexes (sensible profiles) stand in for complexes of qualia. Just as for the qualia realist, qualia complexes are phenomenal characters, so for the property representationalist, sensible property complexes are phenomenal characters. And just as, according to the qualia realist, qualia are the qualities of which we are aware when we introspect, so for the property representationalist, it is the properties comprising sensible profiles.

On this version of property representationalism, accuracy conditions for *visual* experiences appeal to sensible profiles and viewpoints. For example, if person, P, sees two objects, a and b, P's visual experience is accurate just in case there is an ordered triple $<a,b,v>$ that has the relevant property complex[18] and P occupies viewpoint v and a and b are objects of which P is aware. Where there are no objects seen, no question of accuracy or inaccuracy arises.

The earlier comparison of visual experiences with instruments fails to capture the complexity just discussed. A model that does a better job here is that of pictures. Let me explain briefly.

Consider the real-world scene shown in Figure 3 of a triangle and a square, as seen from a particular point of view. Call the triangle 'A' and the square 'B'.

Suppose you tell me to create a realistic picture of this actual scene, from that point of view. Here is my picture (in Figure 4):

My picture is not a good one. It does not accurately depict the real actual world scene. Why not? Well, it gets B wrong. We can put the situation representationally this way: overall, the picture represents A and B as jointly instantiating a certain property complex that they don't instantiate, that of

Figure 3.

---

[18] There is a delicate issue in metaphysics I skate over here. If items, a, b, ... jointly have property P, is the bearer of P really an ordered n-tuple of a, b, ...? If John and Jane jointly lift a piano, is it really an ordered pair of John and Jane that has the property of lifting a piano?

Figure 4.

being a triangle to the left of a parallelogram. But suppose this picture is something I create on my own without it being a picture of any particular real, actual scene. Then no question of accuracy or inaccuracy arises, even if there is a triangle to the left of a parallelogram so that the property complex is instantiated.

Why? Well, it is a bit like the instrument case though more complicated. As far as accuracy conditions go, a picture represents with respect to the objects pictured that they instantiate a given property complex. This is why, where the picture is not a picture of any real objects, no question of accuracy conditions arises. But when there are pictured objects, there is singular content and with singular content, there are accuracy conditions.

My proposal, then, is that visual experiences represent in something like the way that pictures do. This proposal fits with some claims that have been made by well-known cognitive psychologists about both vision and imagery.[19] It also fits nicely with the representational richness of visual experiences. Their richness is like the richness of pictures. Of course, there are important differences between pictures and visual experiences. A realistic picture depicting a blue ball, for example, has a blue part representing the color blue, while a visual experience of a blue ball does not. But what matters here is that visual experiences have features that represent colors and other visible properties (features that are not them-selves colors, for example) and parts that represent things pictured and also that they have a general representational structure similar in important ways to that of pictures.

More specifically, a plausible view is that, at the most fundamental level, visual experiences have the structure of *arrays*, as understood in computer science, where these arrays are made up of cells that are dedicated to lines of sight in the field of view and that contain symbols (that is, simple, primitive representations) themselves dedicated to representing local features on those

---

[19] See, for example, Stephen Kosslyn 1994, Kosslyn et al. 1995.

lines of sight, for example, the color of a tiny surface patch lying there, its distance away, and whether there is part of an edge on it. On this view, visual experiences have a basic matrix-like structure (not accessible introspectively, given what was said earlier).[20] This matrix structure makes them significantly like realistic pictures structurally (and also maps).[21] Where global features and objects are also represented by experiences (as is usually the case), this is a consequence of further processing. My experience of a red, square object, for example, represents both an object and a shape, and neither of these are represented by any symbol within an array cell (unlike the color red). What happens here, we may conjecture, is that a label for the shape is appended to a group of cells in the array, themselves marked out collectively as indicating the presence of an object, on the basis of processing of edges and their locations relative to one another.

---

[20] In a computer array, cells with adjacent addresses need not be physically adjacent. The same can be true for visual experiences on the matrix/array view. The important point for the thesis that visual experiences are picture-like is that visual experiences be at least *functional* arrays or matrices so that adjacent cells have addresses that make them adjacent for processing but they need not be physically adjacent in the brain. In saying this, I do not wish to deny that many visual experiences have an extra layer of complexity that involves the application of concepts. Seeing something as a telescope involves additionally subsuming the seen thing under the concept *telescope*.

[21] The hypothesized matrix structure for visual experiences, under suitable further elaboration, can also be used to explain what have been called "the laws of appearance" (Pautz 2020). Here are some examples of these laws. It is impossible for there to be visual experiences with any of these kinds of content:

    i. Something is pure blue and also greenish blue.
    ii. Something is spherical and cubical.
    iii. Blue is intrinsically overall more like green than purple.
    iv. [That thing is round and green and directly ahead] or [It is square and purple and 45° to the left].
    v. Only: that is cubical [from no point of view].
    vi. A is red all over and B is wholly behind A.

These laws are a little rough and ready and require some qualification, minimally adding "at the same time and place" and (i), for example, needs to be restricted to "same region". As Mark Sainsbury has pointed out to me, we also need to make room for Escher drawings and the Penrose triangle.

My point in the present context is that the structure of pictures, *qua* representational vehicles, as elaborated in the text, prevents them from representing any of (i)–(vi). For example, the reason why nothing can look to be both pure blue and bluish green is that for each cell, there is only a single symbol dedicated to color and if the symbol represents one color on a given line of sight, it cannot simultaneously represent another there. Similarly, something cannot look both cubical and spherical because that would require inconsistencies in how the symbols in cells represent edges; and so on.

3.10 Objections and Clarifications

Objection 1. Awareness and representational content: granting visual experiences have representational contents, can't their subjects be aware *of* those contents? Further, if I have a visual experience of a red square, can't I be aware by introspection of the property of representing a red square? And isn't this property an intrinsic property of the experience?

Reply. Awareness 'of' the content/representational properties of an experience is like awareness 'of' the content of a thought. It is fact-awareness. If I think that 7 is my lucky number and I introspect, I am aware *that* I am thinking that 7 is my lucky number. I am aware that what I am thinking is that 7 is my lucky number. Correspondingly, if I have an experience of a red square and I introspect, I am aware *that* I have an experience of (as of) a red square.

Recall the earlier example of the muffins in the oven. I am not aware of the property of being cooked; I am not conscious of it. But when the timer dings, I am aware that the muffins are cooked. Fact awareness can occur without thing or property awareness.

Objection 2. The argument represents "an error in philosophical method".

> Looking at a blue wall is an easy thing to do, but it is not easy (perhaps not possible) to answer on the basis of introspection alone the highly
>
> theoretical question of whether in so doing I am aware of intrinsic properties of my experience.   (Block 1990, p. 689)

Reply. It seems pretty easy to me. Besides, what's so highly theoretical here? The notion of an intrinsic quality needs to be explained (on Harman's version of the transparency thesis). That's all. Not even this much theory is needed on my version.

Objection 3. "Harman relies on the diaphanousness of perception" (Moore, 1922).

> ... As a point about attention in one familiar circumstance—e.g., looking at a red tomato, this is certainly right.... But attention and awareness are distinct, and as a point about awareness, the diaphanousness claim is both straightforwardly wrong and misleading.   (Block 2001, p. 7)

Block continues:

> One can be aware of what one is not attending to. For example, one might be involved in intense conversation while a jackhammer outside causes one to raise one's voice without ever noticing or attending to the noise until someone comments on it—at which time one realizes that one was aware of it all along.   (Block 2001 p. 7)

So, Block thinks that one is aware of the experience when one views the tomato and introspects. It's just that it's in the background—like the jackhammer.

Reply. Agreed: attention and awareness are indeed distinct. Still, if one is aware of something, in standard visual cases, one *can* attend to the relevant thing directly on the basis of that awareness even if one does not do so. One can switch one's attention/mental focus to the relevant thing directly on the basis of one's overall awareness. But the transparency point is that one can't do this in the experience case. Why? Because one isn't aware of the experience at all. As noted earlier, this is all the argument from transparency based on attention needs.

Objection 4. "[C]lose your eyes in daylight and you may find that it is easy to attend to aspects of your experience. If all experiences that have visual phenomenology were of the sort one gets with one's eyes closed while awake in daylight, I doubt that the thesis that one cannot attend to or be aware of one's experience would be so popular." (Block 2001, p. 8).

Reply. What about cases of normal perception? Stoljar puts the point nicely:

> ... even if Block is right about closing one's eyes in daylight, orgasms and so on, Harman *still* seems to be right about experiences which uncontroversially have intentionality, such as experiences of color. But surely the qualia realist does not want to be maneuvered into the position of saying that color experiences lack qualia. It would be an odd sort of position indeed which postulates qualia but then adds that qualia are only instantiated in cases in which you face the sun with closed eyes, or else are in states of sexual climax!   (Stoljar, 2004)

Further, even in Block's cited cases, one is not aware of aspects of one's experiences (or so I have argued elsewhere (Tye 2000)). One is aware of qualities represented by those experiences (qualities that need not be instantiated). The same is true for other cases due to Boghossian and Velleman (1989), Peacocke (1983), and many others (see Tye 2003).

Objection 5. If projectivism about color is true, then colors are intrinsic properties of experiences that are mistakenly projected onto the world. In that case, we are aware of intrinsic properties of our experiences even though we are not aware of them *as* intrinsic properties of our experiences.

Reply. Projectivism is not true. My experience of blue is not itself blue. Colors, by their nature, are properties of spatially extended surfaces, films, and volumes, if they are properties of anything at all. And they are presented as such in perception.

Objection 6. Isn't the sense-datum theory a version of qualia realism? If it is, then qualia are properties of objects of experiences (namely sense-data). So, the transparency argument doesn't undermine one version of qualia realism.

Reply. Sense-data are usually taken to be mental objects (though not always). If sense-data are mental entities then the sense-datum view is incompatible with the further claim that in normal perception the properties of which we are aware when we introspect are presented to us as mind-independent, unless, of course, there is radical error in normal perception (Martin 2002). Shape, for example, is presented as belonging to an external surface; likewise color.[22]

Alternatively, if sense-data are taken to be non-mental objects then if their qualities are held to be qualia, some qualia are non-mental. This is incompatible with qualia realism, as normally understood. And sense-data, conceived of as non-mental entities, face other problems. For example, where are they located? In the same space as physical objects? How is this possible?

Objection 7. Experience has no presence to us distinct from the presence of its objects... You can see a bush at the end of your street and think nothing of it. But you can also look at the bush, and, in so doing, think about your current situation as a perceiver. In the second case... you are aware of your experience. But in this case, you will not be aware of your experience as a phenomenologically distinct item. Your experience won't

---

[22] I'm inclined to think that both shapes and colors are experienced as intrinsic properties of surfaces and so not dependent on things outside those surfaces including minds.

suddenly pop onto the stage, in a way that might make you say, "Oh, there it is!". You won't be able to selectively focus on your experience, as opposed to the object of the experience, the bush. Experience simply doesn't have that sort of profile.   (Kennedy 2009, p. 587)

Reply. You can certainly think about your current situation as a perceiver as you see the bush. Still, in the given case, (I would say) your experience itself is like the perfectly camouflaged moth. You aren't aware *of* it (de re), period. Rather you are merely aware *that* you are having an experience of a bush. That's why experience has no presence to us over and above its objects.

Objection 8. This objection pertains to transparency and non-veridical perception. It is put as follows by Charles Siewert:

[You cannot attend to what is not there]. Tye often speaks in ways that suggest that [in non-veridical cases] certain [un-instantiated] qualities themselves are to be construed as objects of attention... But if this is what allegiance to the transparency claim demands, we say, at this point the claim hardly seems introspectively evident. Followers of Meinong or Brentano might construct yet other accounts, having me attend to nonexistent or mentally inexistent circular objects.   (Siewert 2004, p. 21)

Reply. This is a large topic. Agreed: you cannot attend to what is not there. But on my view there *is* an un-instantiated quality there in the bad cases. That's how Mary can come to know what it is like to experience red even if she is hallucinating when she leaves her black and white room—in that scenario, she still gets a good 'look' at redness (Hawthorne and Kovakovitch 2006). Is not this introspectively evident to Mary (contra Siewert)? Meinong is committed to there being something that does not exist in the hallucinatory case. No such consequence follows, if we suppose that an un-instantiated quality is present in hallucination.

Further, it is very easy to explain how one could represent a color that is not instantiated in hallucination. Consider the case of a speedometer reading 60 mph when the car is going some other speed or even when the car chassis has been disconnected from the wheels and the speedometer is being artificially tested. On the Normal tracking account of instrument representation, in its simplest form, X represents that P just in case, under Normal (Design) conditions, X is tokened if and only if P and because P. Under Normal conditions, the speedometer would read what it does just in case it is going 60 mph and because it is. But Normal conditions do not obtain; there is misrepresentation. The property of traveling 60 mph is locally un-instantiated. If we think of the senses as instruments provided to us by Mother Nature, we can give a corresponding account of property represen-tation during hallucinations. Even granting that the Normal tracking account of sensory representation is too simple, as stated, the general point still stands (Tye 2000).

Awareness-of is a form of de re representation: sensory representation. If the pointer can do it for speed, why can't we, or rather goings on in our brains, do it for color and other visual qualities? Those who aren't keen on un-instantiated qualities often think of qualities as tropes. There is no trope in the hallucinatory case but there is in the good cases. But just what is a trope? I follow Fine (1999) in thinking of tropes as *qua*-entities (rigid embodiments)—universals under the description of being possessed by such-and-such an object. So, if there are tropes, then there are universals. And if there are universals, why not un-instantiated ones?

Here is a further argument for my view in the case of hallucinations. Suppose that Frank Jackson's Mary has a cousin, Mary*, who, like Mary, is locked in a black and white room. Unlike Mary, Mary* has incomplete knowledge. She doesn't know all the color facts in her room. She comes out and hallucinates something red next to something orange and some-thing green. On the basis of her experience she gains the knowledge that red is more like orange than green (Johnston 2004). Doesn't that require that she be aware of red, of orange, and of green?[23]

You might reply that in hallucinating she is aware of the fact that red is more like orange than green and that this fact-awareness grounds her knowledge (Pautz 2007). But how does she get that fact awareness? Fact awareness is either secondary or primary. If fact awareness is primary, she must be aware of each of the three colors and their resemblance relations. If it is secondary, then what is the fact of which she has primary awareness (or the items of which she has primary awareness)?

Not the fact that *there is* (before her) a red thing that is more similar in color to the orange thing than to the green one. Nor the fact that *everything* red is more similar in color to everything orange than it is to anything green. It is implausible to suppose that she has primary awareness of that general

---

[23] You might object that Mary* would (might) not yet have the concepts red, orange, and green and so would not (might not) know the fact in question. The use of these color concepts is not crucial to the example. Mary* would certainly know that this color is more similar to that color than to that other color.

fact as she hallucinates. The only remaining alternative, it seems to me, is to hold that Mary*'s fact awareness is based on her de awareness of the (un-instantiated) qualities, red, orange, and green.

Objection 9. According to the property representationalist, mind-independent particulars play no role in phenomenal character. But if they play no role in phenomenal character, then, it seems, they play no constitutive role in conscious experience. There's the phenomenal character and then lying behind it in normal cases the ordinary, manifest objects. That's implausible. If we are to respect the commonsense position of naive realism then ordinary objects must enter into normal visual experiences. They must be constituents of those experiences. If ordinary objects merely lie behind conscious experiences, then a veil of perception has been erected.

Reply. The key point to appreciate is that conscious experience can *outstrip* phenomenal character. In the good cases, we are aware of ordinary objects and the properties they instantiate. But we are not aware of either *by* being aware of the other. The experiences we undergo in such cases are partly constituted by the objects we see (Kennedy forthcoming). By contrast, when we are hallucinating, there is no object to enter into the conscious experience. Thus, seeing a tomato (that looks red, round, and bulgy) and hallucinating a ripe tomato are two *different* experiences with a common phenomenal character. So, there is no veil of perception.

Objection 10. What is true is only that our experiences are weakly transparent:

Weak Transparency: it is *difficult* (but not impossible) to attend directly to our experience, i.e., we can most easily attend to our experience by attending to the objects represented by that experience.

(Kind 2003, p. 230)

Weak transparency is compatible with qualia realism.[24]

When we consider paradigmatic examples of transparent objects from everyday life, such as panes of glass, there is no question that the sense of transparency in question must be weak transparency (and thus, that weak transparency must be sufficient to capture the notion of transparency). The

---

[24] See also Van Gulick (1993) and Loar (2003). According to Loar, if we adopt an attitude of "oblique reflection" to our experiences, we can be aware of, and attend to, visual qualia. This, he grants, is not the normal attitude.

window next to my desk overlooks the roof of my neighbor's house. As I look out the window, it is difficult for me to avoid seeing right through it to my neighbor's roof, but it is by no means impossible for me to do so. If I angle my head just so, or if the light is right, I can undeniably focus on the pane of glass of the window itself.   (Kind 2003, p. 233)

Reply. It is hard to see why the fact that objects we usually classify as transparent are weakly transparent shows that "weak transparency must be sufficient to capture the notion of transparency." In reality, glass is not transparent; it is *nearly* transparent. Here is a standard scientific description:

A transparent physical material shows objects behind it as unobscured and doesn't reflect light off its surface. Clear glass is a nearly transparent material. Although glass allows most light to pass through unobscured, in reality it also reflects some light. A perfectly transparent material is completely invisible. (http://www.opengl.org/archives/resources/faq/tech nical/transparency.htm)

My claim is that experiences and their qualities are perfectly transparent. Kind gives no good reason to contest this. She thinks that experiences are like panes of glass and so are nearly transparent. I think that experiences are like perfectly transparent materials.

Interestingly, Kind's claim that we usually, *but not always*, attend to our experiences by attending to their objects and the qualities of those objects is denied by other opponents of transparency. Nida-Rumelin (2007), for example, says

...a person who focuses attention on the intrinsic phenomenal character of her own color experience does so by carefully attending to the color the perceived object appears to have in her experience.   (2007, p. 434)

There is no 'usually' or 'typically' hedge here. Nida-Rumelin takes it that we can focus attention on our color experiences and their phenomenal character and that when we do so we do it (in every case) by attending to the color experienced. Nida-Rumelin continues:

How could somebody think otherwise?...In carefully attending to the color the sky appears to have in one's experience (while wondering for instance if it is slightly reddish or slightly greenish or pure blue) we attend to a specific aspect of the phenomenal character of our own color experience. We attend to the phenomenal character of our experience and we also attend to the color on the surface of the object. There is no conflict between these two acts of attention, rather one might say: there are no *two* acts of attention involved. To attend to the intrinsic character of one's color experience *is* to attend in a particular way to the color the perceived object appears to have.   (2007, p. 434)

Nida-Rumelin takes these remarks to undercut transparency, as understood by myself and Harman. However, there seems to me much that is right in the above passage. And, contrary to Nida-Rumelin's intentions, her remarks (with only small changes) can be used to provide an argument against qualia realism and indeed for property representationalism.

3.11 An Argument for Property Representationalism

Agreed:

(19) In carefully attending to the color the sky appears to have in one's experience (while wondering for instance if it is slightly reddish or slightly greenish or pure blue), one attends to a specific aspect of the phenomenal character of our own color experience.

(20) There is only a single act of attention here.

One doesn't (and can't) turn their attention *away from* the experienced color *to* the relevant aspect of the phenomenal character. Now,

(21) If indeed there is only a single act of attention, then, if there are qualia, that act has two different properties as its objects: the color outside, as it were, and the color quale of the experience.

But one cannot attend to one quality *by* attending to a quality with a different (non-overlapping) bearer (even though sometimes one can attend to one thing by attending to a part of that thing). So, if a single act of attention takes in two qualities of things without common parts, that act must be such that it can be narrowed to just one of those qualities, whether or not the resultant act is to be counted as the same act or not. So,

(22) If a *single* act of attention can be distributed among two or more properties with different non-overlapping bearers, then, for each property, the subject can *narrow* her attentional focus to that property and ignore the other.

But in the introspective case, one can't narrow one's attention in the above way—one can't attend to the phenomenal character of one's color experience without attending to the color experienced.

So,

(23) There is no color quale.

So,

(24) In reality there is just one thing attended to here, the color experienced.

So,

(25) The color experienced *is* the phenomenal character of one's experience.

But

(26) The color experienced just is the color represented in one's experience.

So,

(27) The color represented in one's experience is the phenomenal character of one's color experience.

For the property representationalist, then, if color is out there in the world or at least is presented as such, then so is color phenomenal character. The phenomenal character of a color experience is not an intrinsic quality of the experience. Indeed, it is not a quality of the experience at all. Instead, it is a quality represented by the experience, rather as the meaning of a predicate is not a quality of the predicate but a quality represented by the predicate. Once again, qualia realism is seen to be false.[25]

---

[25] Mark Johnston writes, "There are no qualia. It is ordinary qualities and complexes involving them that account for the so-called subjective character of experience" (2004, p. 146). Even though Johnston is not a representationalist, this claim is one I accept.

3.12 Moore and the Missing Ingredient

I hold the following theses:

Phenomenal Character and Experience: all experiences have a phenomenal character.

Representational Content and Experience: not all experiences have a truth-evaluable representational content.

Common Phenomenal Character: veridical, illusory, and hallucinatory experiences can sometimes have the very same phenomenal character.

Property Representationalism:

a) Necessarily, experiences representing the same property complexes have the same phenomenal character.[26]

b) The introspectable qualities taken by the qualia realist to be qualities *of* experiences (qualia) are really qualities *represented* by experiences.

c) The specific phenomenal character of an experience (that which distinguishes it phenomenally from other experiences) is the property complex represented by the experience.[27]

None of the above theses has anything to say about consciousness or experience itself. Is that transparent to us? At the start of this chapter, I claimed that we are not (de re) aware introspectively of our experiences or any of their properties. From this, it follows that we are not (de re) aware introspectively of the property of being an experience or being a conscious state. Take for example, the experience of red. When we introspect, we are aware of the color red. That is the specific phenomenal character of the experience. By being aware of it, we are aware that we are having an experience of red. But what about the property of being an experience itself? That is not an object of our de re introspective awareness, it seems. But we know that it is there. So, what is it?

In the first passage quoted in this chapter, Moore wrote:

> . . . . that which makes the sensation of blue a mental fact seems to escape us; it seems, if I may use a metaphor, to be transparent—we look through it and see nothing but the blue . . .   (Moore1903, p. 446)

---

[26] (a) is a supervenience thesis. The necessity to which it refers is metaphysical.

[27] What makes that property complex a specific phenomenal character is precisely that it is a complex represented by an experience. For more here, see Chapter 4, p. 9.

Moore then added the following:

> Yet it (consciousness) can be distinguished if we look enough, and if we
> know that there is something to look for. My main object in this paragraph
> has been to try to make the reader see it; but I fear I shall have succeeded
> very ill.

It is not clear exactly what Moore is getting at here. But the point I wish to
make is this. If I introspect my experience of blue, I am aware only of the
color blue. I know, of course that I am having an experience, indeed, an
experience of blue. But that which makes my experience an experience, that
which makes it a phenomenally conscious state, escapes my de re awareness.
I am not aware of it as I am aware of the color blue. I am aware *that* I am
having an experience but I cannot attend to, or be aware of, the property that
makes my experience an experience. That is hidden from my introspective
gaze, so to speak, even though I am aware that it is present, notwithstanding
the truth of the thesis of transparency as elaborated earlier.

It is time to return to the paradox with which we started and the question
of the nature of consciousness itself.

4

Representationalism and Panpsychism

The paradox of consciousness with which we started this book was as follows:

1) Consciousness is either sharp or vague.
2) If consciousness is sharp, then it isn't a (broadly) physical phenomenon.
3) Consciousness is a (broadly) physical phenomenon.
4) *Consciousness is vague* (from 1, 2, 3).
5) If consciousness is vague, then there are possible borderline cases of consciousness.
6) There are no possible borderline cases of consciousness.
7) *Consciousness is not vague* (from 4, 5, 6).
8) *Consciousness is both vague and not vague* (from 4, 7).

The most promising *initial* response to the paradox, in my view, is to accept that consciousness is sharp and to deny premise (2): consciousness is both sharp *and* broadly physical. I say "initial" here since the response, even though it is pointing in the right direction, will need to be revised shortly.

To accept this response is to accept, for reasons given earlier, that consciousness cannot have emerged. But if consciousness did *not* emerge, it was always there. On this view, consciousness itself is a fundamental feature of the micro-parts of physical reality—one of the quiddities—and thus panpsychism is right after all at least to this extent. Through the looking glass, then, we go.

If we adopt the above view, we can agree with dualists that the usual reductive physicalist and functionalist theories do indeed leave something out. As Sydney Shoemaker once put it, even those of us who are physicalists remain dualists "au fond". I think that if we are being completely honest, we will appreciate what Shoemaker was getting at here. There just does seem to be *something* missing in reductive physicalist and functionalist accounts, notwithstanding all the attempts to explain away the nonreductive intuition.

We who are physicalists have tried to live with our attempts, but the paradox with which I started is, I believe, the final nail in the coffin.

To grant that this is the case is not to give up physicalism with respect to consciousness, as noted in Chapter 2. It is rather to relocate it. This relocation does not require us to agree that consciousness is ubiquitous, that rocks and trees are conscious, as some panpsychists hold. Nor is it to accept that at the most fundamental level, there are different species of consciousness, different phenomenal quiddities, as Russellian monists hold. There is, on the above view, *just* consciousness at the bedrock of reality. It is part of the nature of the basic physical entities. All fundamental entities have it. Of course, it is no part of this view that consciousness is a part of microphysics. What theories in microphysics do is to tell us about the relational/structural properties of matter. They leave open the intrinsic nature of the categorical bases for these properties.[1] Consciousness, thus, is physical and fundamental without being in the domain of microphysics.

This view must solve three problems. They are as follows:

1) *The problem of undirected consciousness*: how can the fundamental micro-entities be conscious without being conscious of something or other? How can there be consciousness without content?
2) *The problem of combination*: if not all complex states are conscious, how did the ones that are conscious become so? What combination of fundamental conscious entities did the trick?
3) *The problem of tiny psychological subjects*: are the fundamental micro-entities tiny, conscious people? If not, how can consciousness be part of their nature?

I argue in the first section that the way to solve the problem of undirected consciousness is to draw a distinction between consciousness and what I call "consciousness*" and to hold that it is really consciousness* that is undirected and found in the micro-realm. This requires a revision in the initial endorsement of panpsychism with respect to consciousness. In its place, I propose a more qualified, hybrid position that combines one important aspect of panpsychism with representationalism. This, in turn, requires a modification in the initial response to the paradox. In the next three sections, I argue that the remaining two problems can also be overcome

---

[1] See here Chapter 2.

by the proposed view. In the final section, I address the question of the causal efficacy of consciousness, given the views developed in the earlier sections.

4.1 The Problem of Undirected Consciousness

Representationalism is the thesis that experiences that represent the same property complexes are phenomenally the same. This view is consistent with the view that some experiences do not represent anything. What it requires is that experiences that do not represent anything (and thus are representationally identical) be phenomenally alike. How can this be?

The obvious answer is that some states have the property of being a phenomenal state without having any property of the type: being a phenomenal state that represents R. Furthermore, where state S and state S' meet this condition, they must be the same phenomenally: what it is like to undergo the one must be the same as what it is like to undergo the other.

Here is a parallel. Suppose that it is held that necessarily all proper names that have the same referent have the same meaning. Evidently this is compatible with also holding that some proper names have no referent, for example, 'Vulcan', as used by Le Verrier for a small planet he mistakenly hypothesized to exist between Mercury and the sun in order to explain certain perturbations in Mercury's orbit. What is required to reconcile these two claims is the further view that all proper names which have no referent (thereby having the same referent) have the same meaning.

So, representationalism does not *rule out* the possibility that there are states that are experiences—phenomenal states—that do not represent anything. What it requires is that such experiences be phenomenally identical. Of course, we ourselves are not the subjects of such states. *Our* consciousness is always directed; and the best account of that directedness is that our conscious states always represent. Sometimes, what they represent is extremely impoverished, as when we experience silence (the absence of sound) and nothing else. But usually our experiences have a very complex and multi-faceted representational content, one that is impossible to put fully into words. This is put very nicely by Richard Heck in the following passage:

> Before me now, for example, are arranged various objects with various
> shapes and colors, of which, it might seem, I have no concept. My desk

exhibits a whole host of shades of brown, for which I have no names. The speakers to the sides of my computer are not quite flat, but have curved faces; I could not begin to describe their shape in anything like adequate terms. The leaves on the tree outside my window are fluttering back and forth, randomly, as it seems to me, as the wind passes over them—Yet my experience of these things represents them far more precisely than that, far more distinctively, it would seem, than any characterization I could hope to formulate, for myself or for others, in terms of the concepts I presently possess. The problem is not lack of time, but lack of descriptive resources, that is, lack of the appropriate concepts.   (2000 pp. 489–90)

The picture we naturally have, drawing upon our own experience, is one of conscious states that differ greatly in their content both in our own lives and in those of other creatures. Our conscious states are usually incredibly rich in their content, but as creatures become simpler and simpler, we imagine them undergoing conscious states that are less and less complex until suddenly the light of consciousness goes out for them, the switch turns off.

This picture requires that we think of consciousness as sharp, as does reflection on our own case. There can be indeterminacy in what we experience, in the content of our experience, but not in experience itself (as argued in Chapter 1). Consciousness itself is an on/off matter, but content allows shades of grey. We must draw a distinction, then, between consciousness and the content of consciousness. The vagueness of the latter is secured, on the representationalist view, by its representational character, since representation allows possible borderline cases.[2]

With quarks, there is no representation. There is no content. There is (on the proposal with which this chapter began) just consciousness. So, in the realm of quarks, if representationalism is true, phenomenal variation is impossible. In our own case, there is both consciousness and content.[3] If you undergo the experience of red, you undergo a state that is conscious and that also represents red. There are thus two components to your conscious state. When you introspect, what you are aware of is the content (more carefully, the properties represented). You are not aware *of* consciousness itself. You are aware *that* you are conscious, of course, and thus you are aware of the fact that you are conscious, but when you introspect an experience, you inevitably 'see' through it and end up being aware of (and

---

[2] For more here, see p. 7.   [3] In between, in rocks and trees, there is neither.

focusing your attention on) the properties of which you are conscious, properties that are not properties of your experience (including the property of being an experience). This was Moore's point.

The initial suggestion, then, is that *our* consciousness has two components to it: consciousness and content. Not so with quarks. The states they undergo are undirected or bare and so are missing a key component of our conscious states. Their consciousness has none of the richness and variability of ours. It does not even have the content of the experience of silence. But quarks are conscious nonetheless.

The immediate difficulty that is faced by the view that there can be bare or undirected consciousness is that it flies in the face of the very natural idea that consciousness is a determinable property; for where a determinable property is instantiated, one of its determinates must be instantiated too. Consider, for example, the determinable property of being colored. If something is colored, it must have a determinate color—red, say. Or consider the determinable property of being red. If something is red, it must be some determinate shade of red. On this view, the suggestion that quarks might token the type *consciousness* without being in some determinate conscious state makes no real sense.

It might be replied that where a state is conscious, it is *usually* a state of a specific conscious sort. Perhaps it is a token of the type, *pain*, or a token of the type, *itch*, for example. But it could be denied that a determinate must always be present. On this proposal, consciousness is *not* a determinable state or property at all. Consider the state of being an experience of red. That, it might be suggested, is conjunctive in nature: the state of being an experience and the state of representing red. The determinable-determinate relation is not like the relation of conjunct to conjunction, where the more specific property is a conjunction of the less specific one and some other distinct property. Determinate properties are not to be understood in conjunctive terms. Red, for example, is not a conjunction of being colored and some other property.

On such a view, we ourselves are built in such a way that whenever we undergo a state that is conscious, that state represents something or other. Necessarily, in being conscious, we are conscious of something or other. But quarks, the building blocks of all else (or so for purposes of illustration I am supposing), are not built in this way.

This provides us with an account of just how consciousness itself can be sharp when the given species of consciousness are not. Each species of consciousness is a case of consciousness of something or other, that is, consciousness that represents something, F. The latter is conjunctive in nature: there is the state of consciousness and the state of representing F. The former conjunct is sharp, admitting of no borderline cases; the latter is vague. Since one of the two conjunctive properties is vague, so is the conjunction.

Tempting though such a view may be, as noted above, it is very hard to understand. The intuitive view surely is that if any subject has an experience, that subject experiences *something or other*. Of course, if a subject undergoes an experience, the subject experiences an experience and in so doing experiences something, but surely, in undergoing an experience, the subject experiences *more* than that. The subject experiences something determinate— anger, fear, pain, a tickle, and so on. Consciousness (experience), it seems, just is a determinable property.

The trouble now is that once we accept the determinable view of consciousness, the paradox is back with us; for if consciousness is always directed, if it always has some content, then, on the representationalist view, it always represents something or other. And where there is representation, there are possible borderline cases. So, consciousness has become vague again.

The solution to this difficulty is to be found in an account Jerry Fodor proposed a long time ago of the nature of belief. According to Fodor (1987), what it is to believe that P is to stand in a certain relation R to a sentence in the language of thought that means that P.[4] Fodor called the relevant relation "belief*". Belief* is not the same as belief; for believing essentially involves content whereas belief* does not. Belief*, on Fodor's view, is a functionally individuated relation. It is worth noting that it is not crucial to Fodor's proposal that belief* be a relation at all. He could equally have held that believing that P is a matter of undergoing an inner sentential representation in the language of thought that has the property of being a belief* and that also means that P (where being a belief* is a functional role property). It is this latter possible version of Fodor's view upon which I wish to draw.

Belief is such that one cannot simply believe. One must believe something or other. Likewise, experience is such that one cannot simply experience. One must experience something or other. Corresponding to the property of being a belief*, itself a property that a state must have, on the second version

---

[4] Other propositional attitudes involve other relations.

of Fodor's view, to be a belief, I hypothesize that there is a property, I shall call "consciousness*'" that a state must have to be conscious. Experiencing something, I propose, is a matter of undergoing an inner state (with a quasi-pictorial structure[5]), a state that has the property of being conscious* and that represents something. Consciousness* is not itself a representational property, nor is it a functional property (as with Fodor's belief*). It is, I hold, irreducible and fundamental. And it is consciousness* that is found at the level of quarks. Quarks are conscious* but not conscious. We are both. In being in a conscious state, we are in a state that is conscious* and that also is representational. For us, consciousness* is a property of certain representations. For quarks, it is not. The states that possess it in the micro-realm are not representational vehicles at all.

Consciousness* is sharp whereas consciousness essentially involves content and thus is vague. When we assert baldly that there are no possible borderline cases of consciousness, we are wrong; but the borderline cases arise via the vagueness of the representational aspect of consciousness. There is no vagueness in consciousness*, the other key element of consciousness.

As far as the paradox goes, then, we should deny premise (6) (and not (2) as suggested earlier). But we should acknowledge that the element of consciousness that distinguishes it from other representational phenomena is consciousness* and *that* is sharp. It is the sharpness of consciousness* that leads us to the view that there are no possible borderline cases of experience *apart from* those connected to what is experienced.

If consciousness* is sharp then for reasons given in Chapter 1, it cannot be a physical property that is found with suitable neurological complexity; nor can it be a nonphysical property that emerges from such complexity. Rather it must be a fundamental physical property, part of the intrinsic nature of the fundamental microphysical entities. It is consciousness* that was always there, even in inorganic matter at the most basic level. Not only are we conscious* but so too are quarks.

Before we return to the problem of undirected consciousness, I might add that this proposal provides a simple answer to a hard question for representationalism. Consider the visual experience of red. What is the specific phenomenal character of that experience? Representationalists can offer a substantive initial answer to this question that respects transparency: the specific phenomenal character of the experience of red is just the color red.

---

[5] See pp. 59–61.

But what makes the color red a phenomenal character? Answer: it must be represented by an experience. But what is an experience? To try to answer this question by appealing to the representational nature of experience is to be threatened by circularity. The view I am adopting faces no such threat. It gives a straightforward answer that involves no further reduction or analysis. Every experience not only represents some property (or property complex) but also (and distinctively) has the property of being conscious*. There is no further story about the nature of the latter property. It is irreducible and fundamental. What makes the color red a specific phenomenal character, we may now say, is simply its being represented by a state that has the property of being conscious*.

In summary, the overall solution I am giving to the problem of undirected consciousness is as follows. Representationalism is true. Necessarily, experiences that are representationally the same are phenomenally the same (same at the level of phenomenal consciousness). There is no such thing as undirected or bare consciousness. Consciousness essentially has a content. But the component of consciousness that distinguishes it from other representational entities is not its content. The component that marks consciousness out as unique is consciousness* and that is not a representational property at all. Consciousness*, unlike consciousness, is sharp. As such it did not emerge. Rather it is an intrinsic, physical property of the fundamental entities in micro-reality. These fundamental entities are not conscious, so there is no puzzle as to how they can be conscious without being conscious of something or other.

Consciousness* is not really a *phenomenal* property of token experiences, of course, since that would make it have a representational character (on the representationalist view). Better to say that it is phenomenal*. Positing consciousness*, as described above, is a key element of my qualified panpsychist representationalism and also a key component of my response to the paradox with which we began.

4.2 The Problem of Combination

Consider a red surface S. Given that S is red, certain parts of S are red. Which parts? Answer: all those that are just visible (and larger). Smaller parts than these are not red. Correspondingly, if a state S' is conscious*, on the present view, certain parts of S' are conscious*. Which parts? Answer: all the fundamental parts, the arrangement of which constitutes S'. Not all parts of S' are conscious*, however; for many complexes are not conscious*, including complex parts of S'. So, what is it about the arrangement of the fundamental parts of S' that makes S' conscious*? And what is it about that arrangement that makes S' conscious, *period*? This is the problem of combination, as it arises for my view.

Sometimes, the problem of combination is put in terms of ingredients. At the base level, there are various fundamental forms of consciousness, totally unlike ours. These ingredients then combine in ways that produce the feeling of pain, the feeling of anger, the visual experience of red, and so on. To think of the problem in this way is to liken it to baking a cake. First, you take the eggs and the flour and the baking powder and the butter and the sugar and the vanilla extract; then you combine them in the right ways and put the resulting mixture in the oven for the right period of time at the right temperature. With the appropriate proportions, you end up with a vanilla cake. Might our consciousness be generated in a similar way?

I think not. For one thing, on the view I am proposing, there is just generic, bare consciousness* at the base level, not multiple sorts of consciousness. To suppose otherwise is to take a view that is unnecessarily complicated and also impossible to reconcile with a general representational approach to the different types of conscious state. Patently, there is no representation at the most fundamental level. So, there is no representational ground at that level for different types of conscious state.

Secondly, the view labels the problem rather than solves it. What is it about this particular combination of ingredients that generates consciousness in us, but not in rocks, for example? With the cake, we can give a detailed account of how the various ingredients combine to form the final product. With us, no such account is in the offing.

To make progress here, let us consider some other cases in which properties of parts get transferred to wholes. Rubik's cube consists of twenty-seven smaller cubes. The discrete manufactured parts are cubes and the shape property they share is transferred to the whole. In this case, it is the spatial arrangement of the parts that makes the whole a cube. With other spatial arrangements, a structure of a very different shape would result or perhaps no overall object at all.

Can this be used to illuminate the case of consciousness* and consciousness? Evidently not directly; for it cannot possibly be that the *spatial* arrangement of quarks in humans is what is responsible for the transference of consciousness* from the parts to the whole. Humans vary enormously in the spatial arrangements of their micro-parts. Further, what is it about the spatial arrangement of quarks in a given human being that makes the human conscious*? Why doesn't the spatial arrangement of quarks in a given rock make the rock conscious*? Like-wise for the case of consciousness. These questions seem unanswerable.

Here is another example. Each dancer in the ensemble of dancers performs gracefully. It doesn't follow that the whole ensemble performs gracefully. It might be that the dancer's movements are out of synch or that the dancers individually are performing very different graceful movements that do not fit well together so that the movement of the whole ensemble is disjointed. What matters again is the arrangement of the parts. With the right arrangement, the property of being graceful transfers itself from the parts to the whole. In this case, it is the aesthetic character of the arrangement of the dancers that crucially makes a difference.

Patently in the case of consciousness* it cannot be that the aesthetic arrangement of the quarks composing me that makes me conscious* as well as the quarks. It seems very doubtful that the quarks perform an aesthetically pleasing 'dance' at the micro-level. But even if they do, there is no reason to think that they do not perform an equally pleasing 'dance' in rocks.

For a third example, consider the case of Boodle's club. Boodle's wants to increase its membership. To this end, it engages in a series of actions. It advertises for new members; it reduces the annual fee; it allows members to bring their spouses to club dinners. The members of Boodle's all want Boodle's to increase its membership too. But in saying that Boodle's wants this result, we are not saying that all its members do. We can easily imagine that only a majority of members want a membership increase and it remaining true that Boodle's wants that too. Alternatively, we can imagine that all the members do agree, but the club perversely has a rule that the club is to pursue an action only if (a) there is a majority of members who agree to that action and (b) it is not the case that there is universal agreement (the club favoring some dissent in all matters).[6] In this case, it seems true to say that Boodle's itself does *not* want a membership increase.

These points (and others of their ilk) show that talk of what the club wants is not reducible to talk of what its members want. Suppose now that

---

[6] Obviously, it does not help to weaken the thesis to the claim that Boodle's has the property of wanting to increase its membership if and only if at least a majority of members wants this; for we can imagine that Boodle's has a governing body and that this body makes decisions for Boodle's independent of how many general members want what the board decides. Similar counter-examples can be constructed to other variants.

Boodle's actually functions in such a way that if a certain goal is wanted by all of its members, it pursues that goal. Suppose also (as above) that all the members want to increase Boodle's membership. Then it will be true to say that Boodle's itself wants to increase its membership. Here, a property (wanting Boodle's to increase its membership) gets transferred from the parts to the whole, given that the whole functions in a certain sort of way.

Some will respond to this example by saying that talk of clubs or corporations or societies having mental states is not to be taken literally. Speaking as if they do is simply a matter of our choosing to adopt the 'intentionalist stance' towards them. In Dennett's words: "...the choice of stance is 'up to us,' a matter of decision, not discovery" (Dennett 1973, p. 239).

One big problem with this instrumentalist view is that we also adopt the intentionalist stance towards human beings. We do so to explain and predict their actions. But corporations, for example, engage in actions just as individual human beings do. They buy back their stock; they open up offices; they bring to market new products. We find it very natural to understand why they are behaving as they are by attributing to them mental states. Likewise for clubs. If we are irrealists about the mental states of corporations and clubs, then should we not be irrealists too about the mental states of human beings? If we are (as Dennett seems to be) then we must accept that beliefs and desires are not really inner episodes that cause behavior. Instead, we must hold that ascriptions of belief and desire are true *simply* in virtue of their doing well in predicting people's behavior from the intentional stance. This proposal runs afoul of the Blockhead example. I and my Blockhead input-output duplicate behave in ways that are well predictable from the intentional stance but we should all agree that Blockhead has no mental life.[7]

Another response to the example of Boodle's club is to say that the reason that there is transfer of a certain mental property from the parts to the whole here, given a certain sort of functioning by the whole, is that the mental property in the example (wanting Boodle's to increase its membership) has a functional nature. Since consciousness*, on the proposed view, has no such nature, the example is irrelevant.

My reply is that the point about transfer goes through even if we take the position that functionalism is false for the relevant mental state (and others like it). The general claim I am making is only that if the members of the club all want something P then it will be true that the club also wants P,

---

[7] The example is due to Ned Block. See his 1981. For a good discussion of Blockhead, see Braddon-Mitchell and Jackson 1996, pp. 114–21.

given certain assumptions about how the club functions. It is perfectly possible to accept that this is the case while rejecting functionalism.

Here is a further example. Consider a play with three acts. Each part of the play—each act—is truly wonderful. It does not follow that the play itself is truly wonderful. The three acts must be connected to one another so as to form a coherent whole. Being so connected, there is transfer. Here the relevant sort of arrangement is a complex semantic one.

For a final case, consider superorganisms. These are organisms that consist of many organisms. A superorganism, for example, a colony of bees, is a living thing, according to biologists. It defends its territory; it uses resources from the surrounding habitat; it reproduces; it dies. Queller and Strassman (2009) comment that "the evolution of organismality is a social process. All organisms originated from groups of simpler units that now show high cooperation among the parts and are nearly free of conflicts." The basic idea here is that once individual organisms function together in a certain sort of social way, they form a further organism. In this case, then, the property of being an organism is transferred from the parts to the whole, and what underwrites the transfer is functional arrangement of the right sort.[8]

These last three examples of transfer are more like the case of transfer for consciousness* than the first two. It is important to appreciate that there remains a difference, however. On the view being proposed, consciousness* does not suddenly emerge at the level of certain physical complexes. To suppose otherwise is to encounter immediately problems of the sort discussed in Chapter 1. Brute emergence for consciousness* just isn't a viable alternative. Consciousness* already exists at the level of fundamental parts. But a corporation can want something without its members, or many of its members, wanting it. Similarly, a play can be wonderful without all of its acts being wonderful. And a complex entity can be an organism without its parts being organisms. Still, in each of these three cases, the relevant property is tokened in a given complex entity *because* it is tokened in parts of that entity and they are arranged appropriately. Take, for example, the case of a play P. That particular play, P, is wonderful because its acts are wonderful and they fit together well. The truth of this claim tracks the truth of the

---

[8] I am not supposing here that the property of being a superorganism is the same as the property of being an organism. After all, the property of being a superorganism is only instantiated in complexes that have organisms as proper parts and this isn't true of the property of being an organism. Still, all superorganisms are organisms, so the property of being an organism is transferred from the parts to the whole.

counterfactual: if the parts hadn't been wonderful or they hadn't fitted together well, P wouldn't have been wonderful.

The same is true, I maintain, in the case of consciousness*. A given complex entity C is conscious* because its fundamental parts are conscious* and they are arranged in the right way. The truth of this claim tracks the truth of the counterfactual that if the fundamental parts of C had not been conscious* or they had not been suitably arranged, C would not have been conscious*. The difference between the consciousness case and the play case is that the above counterfactual holds for every conscious* state at the level of complexes whereas the corresponding earlier counterfactual does not hold for every play. Plays can be wonderful even if not all of their acts are wonderful, but complex entities cannot be conscious* unless their fundamental parts are conscious*. To repeat, brute emergence of consciousness* with complexity is not an option. But not *all* complex entities are conscious*, of course. So, what is wanted for transfer in the case of consciousness* is an arrangement A of the fundamental parts that is not found in all complexes and that supports the counterfactual claim that if the fundamental conscious* parts had not been arranged in way A, then the resultant complex state would not have been conscious*.

The next section offers a general discussion of consciousness at the level of complexes. This discussion is intended to pave the way for my proposal, in the following section, as to the nature of the arrangement A and my solution to the problem of combination.

4.3 Poise and the Global Workspace

Consciousness proper always has a content.[9] This is so, I have argued, because consciousness is representational. Consciousness is also always suitably *poised* to make a cognitive difference. More specifically, experiences stand ready and available to make a direct difference with respect to what is believed/reported, what decisions are made, what is remembered, and how one reasons. This needs fleshing out further before we turn again to the problem of combination.

Suppose you are seeing a bomb. Here your visual experience puts you in a position at least to ask "What is that?" with respect to the bomb (and

---

[9] The same is true for other living creatures that are conscious.

typically to form a belief about what it is). Having formed a belief, you may then reason about your best course of action and perhaps decide to run away, given your desire to stay alive. You may also vividly remember the bomb a little later. Likewise with respect to properties of which you are visually conscious in seeing the object. You are put in a position to ask "What color is that?" and "What shape is that?", for example, and typically to go further, to identify the color and shape and to reason to decisions based upon those identifications.

To switch to the case of bodily sensations, if you are feeling pain in your left leg, your experience puts you in a position to believe that *that* (the focus of your attention in your leg) is bad for you and to decide to move the leg away, given your desire that the pain cease. Your experience also puts you in a position to ask at least "Why does that hurt so much?" or "What's causing that?" In addition, experiences are also introspectable states at least in creatures equipped with the power to introspect. So, experiences play a distinctive role as far as access goes. This is known through a priori reflection.

These points apply even to the case of endogenous depression. Suppose you wake up feeling depressed, though not about anything in particular. Your overall feeling has an impact on decisions you make (on whether, for example, to get out of bed or to go to work) and also on what you believe and say about the world outside and your own mental state (for example, "Life is so pointless and dreary" and "I am so depressed" (or later, "Why was I so down yesterday?")).

Not everyone agrees with these claims. Ned Block (1998), for example, claims that there can be experiences that are deeply repressed and thus are not poised to make any differences of the above sort. He cites the case of someone who was tortured in a red room in his youth and who runs from red rooms later in her life without knowing why as a result of a deeply repressed phenomenal memory image of herself in a red room being tortured. The obvious response to this case is to say that the repressed state is representational but it is not a genuine experience. What it is like subjectively to be such a person is to experience a mixture of fear and dread that lie beyond her comprehension whenever she enters a red room. Intuitively, there is no phenomenal *red* image influencing her behavior.[10]

---

[10] For more, see Tye 2009, 2016.

Experiences at the level of complexes, then, are representational states, the contents of which are *poised* to make a direct difference to what the subject believes and later remembers, how the subject reasons, what decisions the subject makes (unlike the contents of other representational states that arise earlier in the processing that generates experiences).

It is interesting to compare these claims with those made in global workspace theory (GWT) about consciousness. That theory tells us that experiences are informational states that arise in an integrated central workspace (Baars 1988). Experiences are active, informational, or representational states in this workspace, a workspace to which specific cognitive mechanisms have direct access. The contents of experiences are widely broadcast via the relevant mechanisms to systems of reporting, reasoning, remembering, and planning. Unconscious states are not broadcast in this way, but they may elicit other responses. For example, backwardly masked stimuli (that is, stimuli that are presented a very short period of time after other stimuli) cannot be reported on or remembered, but the internal states they elicit can influence cognitive processing, for example, motor responses in reaction time tasks.

Another closely related example is provided by response priming (Breitmeyer and Ogmen 2000; Van Gaal et al. 2012). Here participants are asked to respond to a specific target visual stimulus. The stimulus can be either a diamond or a square (let us suppose). If the stimulus is a diamond, the subjects are asked to press the left key as quickly as possible; if a square, the right. Very shortly before presentation of the stimulus, a prime is presented, itself also either a diamond or a square. It has been found that where the prime is the same as the target stimulus, the response time is faster. Where the prime is inconsistent with the stimulus, the response time is slower. Evidently, the priming is influencing the speed of motor response even though the subjects are unconscious of the prime.

Insofar as the claims of GWT are understood as providing us with a reductive account of the essence of consciousness, they are fundamentally mistaken, in my view. Nonetheless, if GWT is understood simply as offering a characterization of the complex states of the brain that *are* conscious then it is compatible with the proposal I have offered above about experiences at the level of complexes.[11] Admittedly, advocates of GWT have focused on the

---

[11] It is worth noting that advocates of global workspace theory (GWT) sometimes write as if the global workspace is essentially a cortical phenomenon. However, there is nothing in the core of GWT that requires this interpretation. The global workspace is essentially a functionally

case of perceptual experiences in elaborating their view, but there is nothing in the idea of a central space containing active representational states, the contents of which are widely broadcast and thus available for a range of cognitive responses, that rules out a wider interpretation of the theory. In what follows, I shall assume such a wider interpretation. We are now ready to return to the problem of combination.

4.4 More on the Problem of Combination

The states of ours that are conscious, if physicalism is true, are highly complex physical states of our brains, as just noted. These states, in being conscious, function in the manner explained above. Consciousness* is transferred, I want to suggest, from the fundamental parts to certain complex wholes as long as the fundamental parts are arranged so as to form states that play the sort of role assigned to conscious states in GWT. Given this arrangement, transfer occurs and the states that are formed in this way are conscious*. Further, in being conscious* *and* playing the relevant global workspace role, these states are thereby conscious.

Let me explain this a little further. Consciousness at the level of complexes occurs in living creatures and not elsewhere.[12] Consciousness at this level is representational and it makes a difference to how living creatures behave. States that are conscious are poised to produce a range of cognitive responses of the sort adumbrated earlier. There is no brute emergence of consciousness, however. Consciousness is present in a given complex via that complex being conscious* and its playing the sort of role specified in GWT. The complex is conscious* because consciousness* is present in its fundamental parts and they are suitably arranged. This arrangement is one that results in the complex playing the relevant GWT role. So, what underwrites the transfer of consciousness* from fundamental entities to certain complexes is their being organized functionally in the right way. It is because the fundamental parts are conscious* and arranged in this way that the

individuated entity. It may well be true that in humans and other mammals the global workspace is partly or even largely cortical, at least in normal cases. But there is evidence that honeybees have a global workspace (see Chapter 5) and honeybee brains lack a cortex.

[12] I do not mean to preclude here the possibility of consciousness in artificial life. For more here, see Tye 2016.

complex states so formed are conscious*;[13] further, in being conscious* and playing the right role, these states are conscious. This is the first part of my solution to the problem of combination.

One possible worry that might be raised for this solution is that if we hold that the states that are conscious* at the level of complexes are states that play a certain role, then we cannot also hold that consciousness* is sharp, since the relevant roles admit of possible borderline cases. This worry is misplaced, however. Consciousness* is not being identified with any role. Furthermore, there is obviously no difficulty in holding that a sharp property may play a vague role. Consider a determinate shade of red, red_{21}, say. That shade can elicit a range of cognitive responses in creatures attuned to it. The role red_{21}, plays here with respect to these creatures' cognitive lives is vague even though red_{21} itself is sharp.

It is worth adding that nothing in the above proposed solution has as a consequence that every metaphysically possible microphysical duplicate of myself is conscious. Such duplicates will certainly behave as I do; and it seems plausible to hold that they will function just as I do. So, they will have internal states that are poised cognitively in just the ways that mine are (on the assumption that poise is understood functionally). Conceivably, some of these duplicates are not conscious, however. Conceivably, they are structural zombies (to use a description from Chapter 2). How is this conceivable? Well, it is certainly conceivable that the fundamental microphysical parts are not conscious*; for microphysical duplication does not logically guarantee duplication at the level of quiddities. So, it is conceivable that there are beings who are microphysical duplicates of ourselves who are not conscious*. Not being conscious*, these beings are not conscious. So, the view on offer (like that of Russellian Monism) respects the intuition of many philosophers that there is nothing incoherent in the idea of zombies who are microphysical duplicates of ourselves, and thus that zombies are indeed metaphysically possible.

So far, I have tried to explain how it is that consciousness is found in some complex entities and not in others. But I have not said directly how it is that the various feelings and experiences we all undergo arise. What combinations of various stripes of consciousness at the micro-level are responsible

---

[13] Rocks and trees, I maintain, are not conscious, even though their fundamental parts are conscious*, because they do not support internal global workspace states and the arrangement that matters to the presence of consciousness* above the fundamental level (and thereby also consciousness) is a functional organization of the sort demanded by global workspace theory.

for the various conscious states we undergo—the feeling of pain, the experience of red, the feeling of anger? This is the second part of the problem of combination.

It should be clear that from the present perspective the problem, as stated, is a pseudo-problem. There are no *stripes* of consciousness at the micro-level, different combinations of which give rise to different macro-phenomenal states. There isn't even consciousness. Instead, there is just bare consciousness*. The various different macro-states are generated via the various representational contents of the complex conscious* states that are cognitively poised. Different macro-phenomenal states are generated representationally.

An example may help to make this clear. Suppose that a large number of quarks are arranged so as to form a complex state A that itself Normally tracks (and thereby represents) property P. That state A, let us further suppose, is poised to produce cognitive responses apt for property P. So, if P is the property of being red, A puts its subject in a position to produce cognitive responses such as these: asking "What color is that?" with respect to P, believing that *that* is red, where *that* is P, and preferring that color to yellow, if the subject prefers red to yellow. Given that the quarks that are combined to form A are themselves conscious*, consciousness* transfers from them to A; and given that A also represents red, A is a full-fledged experience of red. What is true in this case is true in all cases of macro-consciousness. The various species of consciousness are generated by the different properties and different property complexes that are represented, and it is in connection with this that vagueness intrudes.

Of course, there is much more to say about the nature of representation here; my own view (Tye 2000, 2019) is that in general the basic properties represented by experiences are phylogenetically fixed. We are simply built by nature to feel pain, to experience various colors, to feel anger, and so on. Other creatures are built differently and their experiences are different in varying degrees from ours. The bird that immediately spots what is to us a green caterpillar sitting on a green leaf (and to our eyes almost perfectly camouflaged) does so because it experiences the caterpillar as having a color different from that of the leaf (in my view, the color is a binary one—ultra-violet green, as we might call it—only one component of which is available to us, given the different sensitivity of the cones in our eyes). When we view the caterpillar, the state we are in represents it as green since that state is the one in us that Mother Nature has given us to track the color green. That state is the one that Normally tracks green (or, in Dretske's terms (1988), has as its biological function to indicate green). The bird viewing the caterpillar is in a different conscious state, one that Normally tracks the *binary* color, ultraviolet-green.[14]

However the further details go, I take it that the proposed response to the problem of combination is now clear. To repeat, there is no combination of different micro-conscious states that generates our macro-conscious states. The unanswerable question asked earlier (in Chapter 2) of the Russellian monist, namely: "Why should *these* micro-phenomenal quiddities give rise to *that* macro-phenomenal state rather than *this* one?" has a false pre-supposition. Our "smooth, structured, macroscopic phenomenology" (as Chalmers puts it in his 1995) has no micro-phenomenal basis. Structure arises simply from the structure of the property complexes represented by our experiences. The reason why it seems fundamentally misguided to try to give a micro-phenomenal, combinatorial account of phenomenal pinkness in the case of Sellars' example of the phenomenal pinkness found in the visual experience of a pink ice-cube (also mentioned in Chapter 2) is that phenom-enal pinkness is just pinkness, and that isn't a feature of the visual experience at all. Pinkness is what is represented by the experience. It's as simple as that.

4.5 The Problem of Tiny Psychological Subjects

If consciousness were found at the most fundamental level of physical reality, then it appears that there would have to be tiny subjects of con-sciousness at that level. After all, pains can't exist without a creature that is in pain and neither can itches or feelings of anger or visual experiences of red. Conscious states are necessarily owned. If this is true for specific kinds of consciousness, surely it must be true for consciousness itself. There can't be consciousness without a being that is conscious. Likewise for consciousness* arguably. Quarks, then, on such a view, if they are conscious or conscious*, must be tiny psychological subjects, tiny people, and this is surely absurd.

I agree that this consequence would be absurd, but it does not follow. Consciousness does not require a person who is conscious. Personhood is plausibly tied to rationality. Kant, for example, famously wrote:

[E]very rational being, exists as an end in himself and not merely as a means to be arbitrarily used by this or that will ... Beings whose existence

---

[14] For more here, see Bradley and Tye 2001.

depends not on our will but on nature have, nevertheless, if they are not rational beings, only a relative value as means and are therefore called things. On the other hand, rational beings are called persons inasmuch as their nature already marks them out as ends in themselves.

(Kant [1785] 1998: [Ak 4: 428])

And:

The fact that the human being can have the representation "I" raises him infinitely above all the other beings on earth. By this he is a person....

(Kant [1798] 2010: 239 [Ak 7: 127])

If anything like this view is correct, it is obviously misguided to tie consciousness to persons. *We* have the capacity to step back and ask ourselves whether *our* desires are reasons for acting, whether *our* impulses should be followed. But patently many animals lack this capacity as Kant himself acknowledged ([1798] 2010: 239 [Ak 7: 127]). And it is undeniable that many animals are conscious. Indeed, on the view I have argued for elsewhere, animals as simple as honeybees are conscious. Moreover, humans with advanced Alzheimer's disease or acute autism are unable to reflect rationally in the ways Kant supposed necessary for personhood.

Perhaps it will now be said that what consciousness requires is not a person, but only a creature (an animal) that is conscious, whether or not that creature (animal) is capable of rational reflection. This still seems too strong, however. Why suppose that robots cannot be conscious simply because they aren't animals? One response to this is to say that a suitably constructed robot is still an animal, albeit an *artificial* one. But whether or not this is a useful classification, the key point is that insofar as we are inclined to attribute consciousness to such a robot will depend on whether we are disposed to attribute to it internal states that are cognitively poised to produce a range of cognitive responses of the same general types as those produced by our conscious states. So, if we agree that such a robot will be conscious, patently its consciousness will be directed just as ours is. Its conscious states will represent various properties and, by representing those properties, will be poised to produce beliefs and desires appropriate to them.

On the view I am proposing, it is not consciousness that is found at the most fundamental level, but rather consciousness*, and consciousness* is not directed at all. It is bare, without any content. So, there is certainly no requirement imposed by the presence of consciousness* at that level that the most fundamental entities absurdly be persons or animals (biological or artificial) or beings with cognitively poised internal states.

Is it even required that there be a psychological *subject*, where there is consciousness*? Consider the case of an explosion. We know that explosions can't occur without things that explode. Are things that explode the *subjects* of explosions? Suppose a stick of dynamite explodes. It is a thing that explodes obviously but is it aptly described as the subject of the explosion? I think not. Subjects are sometimes individuals whose responses are studied (as when there are subjects in a psychological experiment); at other times, subjects are dead people undergoing post-mortem study; alternatively, a subject may be the topic of an essay or the object of a work of art or simply a word or expression linked with a predicate in a subject-predicate sentence. But things that undergo changes, as the stick of dynamite does as it explodes, are not well classified as subjects. Nor are things that token longer-lasting states, as with a piece of glass that tokens the state of being brittle.

Likewise, what is required for the tokening of bare consciousness* is simply that there be a thing that is conscious*. Nothing more is necessary. So, the thought that the view being proposed requires that quarks be tiny people or tiny animals or tiny rational beings or tiny subjects is totally misguided. We, with our consciousness, are people, indeed (normally) rational subjects. But there can be consciousness* at the most fundamental level without any person, any rational being, any psychological subject.

4.6 The Causal Efficacy of Consciousness

If conscious states evolved at the level of certain complexes, increasing in their richness with the representational richness of those complexes, we would expect consciousness itself at this level to have causal power, to make a difference. Why else would Mother Nature endow some complex states with consciousness at all? Why not just make them representational? But what does consciousness do? The obvious answer, trite though it is, is that consciousness enables living beings that have it to do all those things that living beings that lack it cannot do.

Here is an example. Flash an 'X' or an 'O' into the blind field of a blindsight subject. You will get no response. Why not? Because the blindsight subject is not *conscious* of an 'X' or an 'O' (Weiskrantz 1988; Marcel 1998). But the blindsight subject is in a state generated by her visual system that represents an 'X' or an 'O'. After all, if you force the blindsight subject to guess what is present, she will usually guess correctly, even though she does not believe her guess. By contrast, if you flash an 'X' or an 'O' before me and ask me which is present, you will get an immediate answer. What is it about my visual state that enables me to produce a response (and believe it)? Answer: my visual state, unlike that of the blindsight subject, is *conscious*. My visual state here, in virtue of being conscious, causes me to respond to the question. The blindsight subject's state, not being conscious, does not have the same effect. So consciousness as such has casual efficacy.

We do not need to appeal to the special and strange case of blindsight subjects to make the point. As noted in section 4.3, stimuli that are briefly presented to subjects, and that are then backwardly masked so as to make them unconscious, may still be processed deeply, with the result that they have high-level content that can prime subsequent behavior. In some of these cases, with slightly different timing and intensity settings, the backwardly masked stimuli may still be visible. Where this happens, the immediate behavior of subjects is very different. (The so-called attentional blink can be arranged similarly; Raymond et al. 1992; Marti et al. 2012.) Why? The obvious answer is that it is the fact that the subjects are conscious of the stimulus in these cases that makes their immediate behavior different.

How is it that consciousness is causally efficacious here? This is the question I want to address in the present section. The order of discussion is as follows. I begin by explaining why it might be thought that if a view of the sort I am proposing is adopted then consciousness at the level of living beings does not really make any difference. It does so by comparing the case of consciousness and verbal behavior, on my view, with that of the soprano and the wine glass (Dretske 1988). Next, I explore the distinction between actions and bodily movements. Using some of these points, it is argued that a satisfactory account is available for understanding how it is that consciousness makes a difference in a range of important cases.

Let us begin with the soprano and the wine glass. The soprano sings "I love you." Her act of singing causes the wine glass to shatter. Her singing is an event made up of a certain sequence of sounds (or so it is usually supposed). Those sounds have various physical properties: a certain pitch, amplitude, etc. They also have the property of meaning *I love you*. The semantic property is not identical with any of the physical properties relevant to this causal sequence nor is it necessitated by them. The semantic property is thereby causally irrelevant, or so it seems reasonable to conclude;

for even if the sounds had possessed a different meaning or they had meant nothing at all, the wine glass would still have shattered (Dretske 1988, p. 79).

Suppose now that my visual experience at time t causes me to say 'Yes, there is an "X"' in response to the presented 'X'-stimulus when I am asked if the stimulus is an 'X'. My visual experience has the property of being conscious, and that property (on the proposed view) is an irreducible physical property, distinct from any of the structural properties found in the physical sciences. I also accept that my visual experience at t is at least *constituted* by a token neural state in my brain. On the face of it, then, the case is not unlike that of the soprano and the wine glass. The sounds produced by the soprano have a physical make-up as does my experience; furthermore, the property of being conscious possessed by my experience has a significant feature in common with the semantic property of meaning *I love you*, namely that if it had been missing, so long as its bearer had retained all the same lower-level physical properties, as specified in the physical sciences, the effect would have been the same. How, then, does the fact that my visual state is conscious make any causal difference to my verbal behavior?

I might add that the dualist about consciousness has a similar worry about causal efficacy. To see this, suppose that we repudiate the assumption above that, at the token level, phenomenal states are constituted by (or identical with) physical states.[15] It remains true that my behavior is caused proximately by activity on the relevant motor neurons. Those neurons fire in response to the activity of neurons inside my brain. If the phenomenal is nonphysical, those cranial neurons could have had exactly the same physical properties without the phenomenal properties being instantiated, and having those physical properties, they would have caused exactly the same activity on the motor neurons, or so it seems highly plausible to suppose. So, I would have behaved verbally just as I actually do. The fact that my state is conscious thus seems causally irrelevant. It makes no difference. Even if it is missing, the same behavior results.

The question, then, for my account is this. On the proposed view of consciousness, how can we *avoid* the charge of epiphenomenalism for consciousness? I turn next to actions and bodily movements.

Consider again the soprano. The soprano's action is not a basic one; for she does it by performing another action, that of moving her tongue and

---

[15] For general discussions of constitution versus identity, see Fine 2003, 2006; Frances 2006; King 2006.

mouth appropriately. By contrast, her moving her tongue is basic. Basic actions are causings of intransitive bodily movements. Transitive bodily movements are such causings. They are the movings of bodily parts, and as such they may reasonably be viewed as *processes* that are productions of the relevant intransitive movements by the agents (Dretske 1988, p. 15).

Basic actions begin with events internal to agents that cause the intransitive movements and end with those movements. Non-basic actions can be understood in a similar way. Smith's killing Jones by stabbing him begins with Smith's act of stabbing and ends with Jones' death, hours or days later. Smith's killing Jones is a process, the production of his death by an act of stabbing. In saying that the soprano does two things, moving her tongue and mouth, and singing an aria, I am saying that there are two processes, one of which incorporates the other. One of these processes consists in the production of certain intransitive muscle movements; the other, wider process consists in the production of certain sounds.

In the soprano case, the sounds that cause the glass to shatter are tokens of words and, as such, have meaning. Their semantic properties, however, are causally irrelevant to the breaking of the glass. The sounds do not cause the glass to break *in virtue of* their semantic properties. Does the soprano's singing the aria itself, then, cause the shattering of the glass? No, it does not. As just noted, her singing is a process, the last part of which consists in the sounds that cause the shattering of the glass. The sounds that cause the glass to shatter are tokens of words and, as such, have meaning. Their semantic properties, however, are causally irrelevant, to the breaking of the glass. The sounds do not cause the glass to break in virtue of their semantic properties.

My visual experience (seeing an X on the screen) causes me to say 'Yes, there is an "X"' when asked if an 'X' is present. So, my visual experience causes a certain action. That action is the production of a certain sound. My visual experience, then, causes a certain process, one that begins with events inside me and ends with a certain sound. The process has a certain intransitive bodily movement (hereafter called 'M') as a proper part. It does *not* follow from this that my visual experience also indirectly causes M. To suppose that it does so follow is either to commit the fallacy of division (by inferring incorrectly that what is true of my action must be true of the parts, in this case movement M) or to argue that my visual experience causes M via the transitivity of causation and the mistaken assumption that the action of my causing M *itself* causes M.

The general picture I want to propose, then, of phenomenal causation is as follows: the actions caused by phenomenal events are processes. These processes include intransitive bodily movements as proper parts. Where phenomenal events cause actions, they typically do so in virtue of their phenomenal properties, including the most general phenomenal property of being conscious. In the case of my saying 'Yes, there is an "X"' when asked if an X is present, my conscious visual state has the property of being conscious and also the property of representing an X. Both properties are causally relevant to my action of saying what I do. That action is a process including an intransitive bodily movement.

I have claimed that the property of being conscious (being a conscious state) is not like the semantic property of meaning *I love you* in the case of the soprano and the wine glass. With the above distinctions in hand, the question still remains as to how, if this is so, consciousness is causally efficacious.

Let us summarize where we are as far as the causal efficacy of consciousness goes. In the soprano example, the relevant effect is a piece of physical behavior, the wine glass shattering. In the consciousness example, the relevant effect is an action, my saying 'Yes, there is an "X"' when presented with an 'X' and asked whether an 'X' is present. It is the fact that my visual state is conscious that is responsible (at least in part) for its causing this action. Why? What is the difference in the consciousness case and just how is the property of being conscious causally active?

In the soprano example, if the sounds had not meant *I love you*, the glass would still have shattered, since what matter here are the pitch and volume of the sounds. By contrast, if my visual state had not been conscious, I would not have responded by saying 'Yes'. That *action* would not have occurred.

In accepting that the property of meaning *I love you* in the soprano/wine glass case is epiphenomenal to the given effect, I am not suggesting, of course, that it is not causally relevant elsewhere. Consider this example. The soprano is in her dressing room with her husband whom she adores. She sings playfully to him 'I love you' and he breaks into a big smile. In this instance, it is true that if the sounds the soprano produces had not meant *I love you*, he wouldn't have broken into a big smile. The intentional action of smiling is triggered by the sounds she produces in virtue of their meaning *I love you*. The physical properties of those sounds are not causally relevant; for had the soprano sung *I love you* louder or with a different pitch, her husband would still have broken into a big smile. In this case, the effect, now a certain action instead of a piece of physical behavior, is caused by the semantic property of the sounds and not by the lower-level, local physical properties.

Something like this is true in the case of consciousness. My action of saying 'Yes, there is an "X"' in response to the question 'Is an "X" present?' is partly a result of my internal token state being conscious; for if that state had not been conscious, I would not have said 'Yes, there is an "X"'. However, my action is *not* a result of my internal state having whatever neural property it has in the actual world (call this property 'N*'); for in the nearest world in which N* is missing, my internal token state is still a conscious state representing the presence of an 'X' (albeit a token state with a different neural constitution) and so I would still have said 'Yes, there is an "X"'.

In making this final observation about N* not being causally relevant my action, I am appealing to the falsity of a certain non-backtracking counterfactual. Some will object to this on the grounds that there are well known counter-examples to counterfactual analyses of causation.[16] For present purposes, it is not necessary to face this much larger issue. My interest here is in showing that consciousness *is* causally efficacious with respect to my action, not that N* is *not*. All that is needed for the former claim is that the truth of the relevant counterfactual provides a *defeasible* sufficient condition for causation.

Perhaps it will now be objected that while it may indeed be true that creatures with consciousness can do many things that creatures without consciousness cannot, there are possible creatures without consciousness that can do everything we do can do. I have in mind here zombies (structural zombies). Such beings (who are alike us microphysically but lacking the quiddity of consciousness* at the most fundamental level) will duplicate all of our actions. So, it has not really been shown that consciousness is causally efficacious with respect to action after all.

This objection is confused. Consider once again my saying 'Yes, there is an "X"' in response to the question 'Is an "X" present?' This is partly a result of my internal token state being conscious for the reason already given. Now it is indeed true that my structural zombie twin would act just as I do; but this is irrelevant to the claim I am making. The fact that a given effect E in the actual world brought about by cause C is brought about in some other metaphysically possible world by a different cause C' does not undermine the legitimacy of C as a cause in the actual world. If it is true that in the nearest possible world to the actual world in which C is missing, E is missing too, that suffices (in the absence of a defeater) to show that C causes E. It is not necessary that in all other metaphysically possible worlds in which C is missing, E be missing too. In the case at hand, the nearest possible world in which my current state is not conscious is one in which the state I am in is

---

[16] For a defense of the counterfactual analysis of causation, see Lewis 1973 and also later (with qualifications), Lewis 2000.

not suitably cognitively poised (and thus, no verbal action results), there being in that world a difference in the *arrangement* of the fundamental parts. The nearest world is not one in which the fundamental entities in physical reality lack consciousness* and everything else remains the same.[17] Consciousness, then, really does make a difference, notwithstanding the existence of metaphysically possible zombie worlds with beings whose actions duplicate ours. And it does so even though consciousness is irreducible and fundamental.

In overall summary, my argument has been that consciousness is not a nonphysical property; rather is it a broadly physical property, the key, distinctive component of which, consciousness*, is found at the most fundamental level of physical reality and also at the level of certain complex physical structures, namely those that are active global workspace states. Consciousness*, I claim, is a broadly physical property with an irreducible nature. What is unusual about consciousness*, what makes it stand out is that it is a sharp, fundamental property that lies outside the domain of microphysics. Since consciousness* is sharp, it has no possible borderline cases and neither thus does consciousness proper (apart from those that arise in connection with its content). The various different conscious states arose gradually (being representational) and it is here that borderline cases are to be found. Mother Nature saw fit to endow certain physical complexes with consciousness, since its presence made a difference. It enabled living creatures that have it to do many things—things that non-conscious living creatures often cannot do at all.

I have tried to show that the view for which I am arguing provides a simple and satisfying solution to the paradox of consciousness with which I began. It also respects the central tenets of representationalism about consciousness while still making consciousness itself special and irreducible within the physical domain. We might call the view "*panpsychist representationalism*". Whatever we call it, it is a view that I now believe better fits all the requirements of adequacy a theory of consciousness needs to meet than any other theory currently available.

---

[17] After all, it surely seems plausible to hold that the intrinsic natures of micro-entities do, in fact, make a difference to how they behave and thus that if they had not been conscious*, they would not have behaved as they do. So, in the nearest world to the actual world in which consciousness* is missing at the micro-level, the behavior of micro-entities is different there and that difference will change the behavior of complex arrangements of such entities.

5

The Location of Consciousness

Consciousness*, as I have called it, is everywhere, residing as it does wherever there is a quark or some other fundamental entity. But what about consciousness? Evidently, consciousness requires a brain. If creatures with brains had never evolved, there would have been no such thing as consciousness. But where in the brain is consciousness located? And which brains support consciousness? I begin with the former question.

5.1 A Hypothesis by Crick and Koch

Francis Crick and Christoph Koch (2005) have speculated that the claustrum, a thin, irregular sheet of neurons attached to the underside of the neocortex, which receives inputs from nearly all regions of the cortex and projects back to nearly all such regions, is the place where information underlying conscious perceptions is integrated into an harmonious conscious whole. They liken the claustrum to a conductor. See Figures 5 and 6.

Some recent work seems to support Crick and Koch's conjecture. Mohamad Kobeissi and colleagues managed to stimulate the claustrum of a female subject and thereby turned her consciousness off and then back on again. To this end, they were using deep brain electrodes, with one of these situated next to the claustrum. The subject here had epilepsy and they were trying to determine where in the brain her epileptic seizures originated.[1]

Kobeissi (2014) found that when they stimulated that region with a high frequency electrical signal, the woman lost consciousness even though she remained awake. She stopped reading, stared blankly ahead, and did not respond to visual or auditory commands. As soon as they stopped stimulating the region by the claustrum, the woman regained consciousness right away and she had no memory of the prior absence of consciousness

---

[1] The subject had an intact corpus callosum.

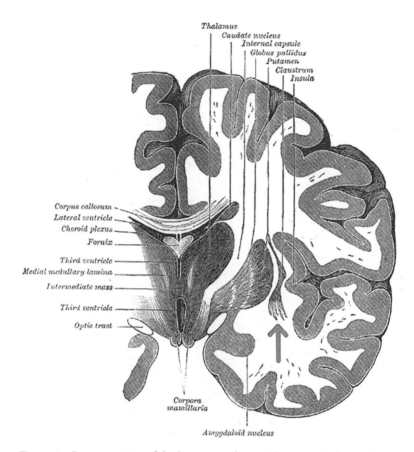

Figure 5. Corona section of the human cerebrum. The arrow indicates the claustrum.

(so they didn't just paralyze her; also she was awake, blinking, etc). Over a course of two days, this procedure was repeated with the same results every time.

To control for the possibility that the woman was simply unable to move or talk as a result of the electrical stimulation of the claustrum, Kobeissi and his colleagues had the woman repeat the word 'house' and snap her fingers just before stimulation started. They found that there was no sudden loss of speech or movement, as would have been the case if the electrical activity was blocking her ability to speak or move. Instead, she gradually spoke more quietly and

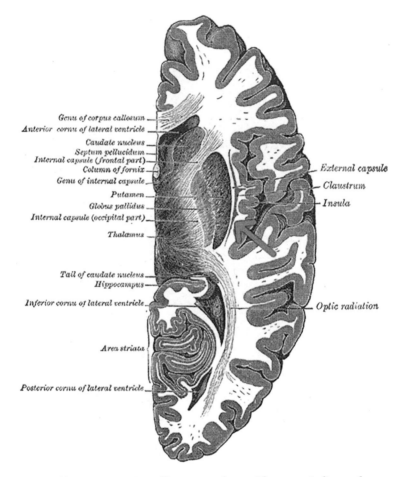

Genu of corpus callosum
Anterior cornu of lateral ventricle
Caudate nucleus
Septum pellucidum
Internal capsule (frontal part)
Column of fornix
Genu of internal capsule
Putamen
Globus pallidus
Internal capsule (occipital part)
Thalamus

Tail of caudate nucleus
Hippocampus
Inferior cornu of lateral ventricle

Area striata

Posterior cornu of lateral ventricle

External capsule
Claustrum
Insula

Optic radiation

Figure 6. Transverse section of human cerebrum. The arrow indicates the claustrum.

moved more slowly until she stopped altogether (again while remaining awake).[2]

Still, Kobeissi's experiment is very far from decisive; after all, the woman was not a typical subject. Furthermore, there is at least one documented case of an adult human subject lacking a claustrum who nonetheless undergoes

---

[2] Why does this occur gradually? Maybe when consciousness is turned off, speech and movement gradually diminish without being reinforced by it.

experiences (Damasio et al. 2013). This subject had his insular cortices and claustrum destroyed as a result of Herpes simplex encephalitis. Yet all aspects of feeling remained intact. According to Damasio, what the case of this subject suggests is that the switch for consciousness is buried deeper than the claustrum, perhaps in the brainstem (which was intact in this patient). He says:

> Is it reasonable to consider that feelings do not arise "first" in the cerebral cortex but actually have their foundation at brainstem level? We believe it is entirely reasonable. It is an established fact that basic homeostasis— hunger, thirst, other drives, metabolic regulation, cardiovascular function— is controlled from the sector that includes the brain stem and the hypothalamus.... Moreover, basic emotions are also executed at this level, from fear and panic to joy (Panksepp 1998).... What we are suggesting here is that besides serving as executors of the machinery of life regulation and emotions, the brain stem region also contains structures capable of generating neural maps of the physiologic states that result from regulatory and emotive responses, thus serving as a platform for the experience of feelings. (p. 149)

The puzzle here is that if the platform for consciousness is at the brainstem level, why in the case of Kobeissi's subject, did consciousness disappear when the claustrum was electrically stimulated and re-appear when it was not?

I turn next to the case of decorticate children and their relevance to the claims made by Crick, Koch, and Damasio.

5.2 Decorticate Children

Decorticate children are children born without a neocortex. The standard view of such children is that while they can be awake, they have no awareness, no consciousness. They do not feel pleasure or pain. At the conscious level, they are mere vegetables.

Bjorn Merker has recently contested this view. After spending several weeks with decorticate children and their families, Merker said the following:

> These children are not only awake and often alert, but show responsiveness to their surroundings in the form of emotional or orienting reactions to environmental events . . . , most readily to sounds but also to salient visual

stimuli ... They express pleasure by smiling and laughter, and aversion by "fussing", arching of the back and crying (in many gradations), their faces being animated by these emotional states. A familiar adult can employ this responsiveness to build up play sequences predictably progressing from smiling, over giggling to laughter and great excitement on the part of the child. (Merker 2007, pp. 1–12)

There can be no doubt that these children are extremely impaired behaviorally. But in addition to apparently showing pleasure, as described above, they also sometimes apparently feel pain, by rubbing an area that has been banged or pinched. This is shown by facial expressions such as wincing, grimacing, and flinching in 14%, vocally in ways such as crying, screaming, and yelling in 78%, and body use such as wriggling, pulling away, and startling in 4% of the children.

Their behavior in response to aversive stimuli, it is worth noting, contrasts sharply with that of Gabby Gingrass, a girl who is one of around 100 people on the planet who genuinely is incapable of feeling pain. Gabby does not react to negative stimuli. For example, she poked out an eye when she was young; she ran into a wall, thereby dislocating a jaw, without anyone realizing that she had undergone a bad injury; she bit through her gums. The behavioral evidence suggests that decorticate children are *not* vegetables.

In some other mammalian species, it is worth noting that the impairment due to the removal of the cortex shortly after birth is much less striking. One of the researchers who reported on such decorticate rats said later:

The thing that stands out, in my memory, is how astonishingly normal these rats were. Without a cerebral cortex, these decorticate rats lacked fine motor control, but in most other respects, they were very similar to normal rats. For instance, we tested them on a test of finding individual pieces of Froot Loops brand cereal that had been hidden in little wells inside a special test chamber. Since they lacked fine motor control, the decorticate rats had trouble picking up the Froot Loops and putting them into their mouths. However, they were pretty good at locating the pieces of cereal. Indeed, I would say that searching for Froot Loops is a purposeful behavior that requires at least some degree of consciousness. It certainly isn't a reflex. If normal rats have consciousness—and there is no reason to think that they don't—then the decorticate rats had plenty of it, too.

(Cox 2005)

These claims about decorticate children and rats may seem to support Damasio's view that the brainstem is the basic platform of consciousness. But if this is the case, we are still left with the question of why it is that electrically stimulating the claustrum of Kobeissi's patient consistently shut down consciousness.

5.3 The Prefrontal Cortex and Working Memory

A widely accepted theory regarding the function of the brain's prefrontal cortex (PFC) is that it serves as a store of short-term memory and thereby guides action.

Information is initially represented by networks of sensory neurons, such as those in the primary visual cortex at the rear of the brain. That information (about, for example, the shape of a rose, its color, its smell, the memory of its significance (for example, a gift on Valentine's day)) is then integrated into a unified whole in normal cases via the claustrum. The integrated information is then passed on to working memory, where it becomes accessible for global broadcasting. On this view, given my earlier claims about which complexes are conscious, reverberating neuronal activity in the PFC underlying such accessibility is the neural basis of consciousness—in many cases.

This picture encourages us to think of the claustrum as a kind of trigger for consciousness, rather as the ignition key in a car is a trigger for the engine's running. And just as the right activity in the engine is what drives the car, so the right activity in the PFC is what drives cognitive reactions at the level of belief, decision making, planning, and reasoning that underlie action. So, the locus of consciousness is not the claustrum but rather the PFC, at least in many cases.

If we think of the claustrum as a trigger in this way, we can explain why consciousness did not cease for Damasio's patient whose claustrum had been destroyed. Consider again a car engine. Normally, turning the ignition key into the 'on' position is what triggers the engine's running. But the engine can be made to run even if the ignition key switch has been destroyed, by, for example hot-wiring it. Likewise, if what really matters is activity of a certain sort in the PFC, the claustrum is not essential. Damasio's patient had normal basic visual perception and widespread activity in the PFC. Some of this activity was produced by activity in the thalamus which also serves to integrate information and with which the PFC also has connections. Damasio, then, was too fast in inferring that the brainstem is the basic platform for consciousness as it is for heartbeat, breathing, and other primitive systems underlying life.

What about the case of Kobeissi's patient? Recall that electrically stimulating the claustrum via a probe inserted next to it had the effect of cutting off activity in the claustrum. Interestingly, activity in the PFC also shut down. So, it may well be that the stimulation of the claustrum sent a message to the PFC to suppress activity there.

As for decorticate children, one response that might be made to such cases is that the children may not have been completely without a cerebral cortex (Watkins and Rees 2007, in reply to Merker 2007). To this Shewmon, Homes, and Byrne (1999, p. 371) say:

> The main point is that these children's consciousness can be inferred to be mediated subcortically *not* because there were absolutely zero cortical neurons, but because the few that were present could not plausibly subserve the *totality* of their conscious behaviors. That is why parents were invariably told—with complete confidence by relevant specialists—that their child would unquestionably remain in a vegetative state for as long as he or she lived. Experienced neurologists, to whom the authors have shown the CT and MRI scans with an invitation to guess the child's level of functioning, also typically predict vegetative state.

Given that the examples adduced by Merker and Shewmon involve congenital brain malformations, one reasonable hypothesis is that developmental plasticity underlies the subcortical mediation of consciousness. In this connection, we should note the following comments from Shewmon, Holmes, and Byrne (1999, p. 371):

> The two children with vision despite fetal absence of occipital cortex had brain malformations arising *earlier in gestation* than the two with no vision despite occipital remnants. Presumably in the latter cases, prior to telencephalic infarction the visual system had developed so that relevant subcortical nuclei were already committed to a functional relationship with occipital cortex whereas in the former the absence of occipital cortex all along allowed these subcortical nuclei "free rein" to organize *optimally* for functional vision. If such vertical plasticity can occur with vision there is no reason to suppose it cannot also occur to some extent with other sensory and motor modalities *and with their mutual interactions mediating adaptive environmental relatedness. i.e. with consciousness.*

It is interesting to note that for those supposedly decorticate children where there is some occipital cortex left, the auditory cortex is almost always completely missing. Yet the vision of the children in these cases is significantly worse than their audition. This fact can be explained straightforwardly using Shewmon's vertical plasticity hypothesis: subcortical nuclei in the auditory case take over the job that would have been done by cells in the auditory cortex had there been any, whereas in the visual case, subcortical nuclei play a subservient role to the remaining cells in the occipital cortex, and the latter cells are typically glyotic or have other functional abnormalities, so vision is poor.

A reasonable suggestion, then, is that activity in subcortical neurons forms the basis for a primitive working memory in decorticate children who show signs of consciousness. These children orient themselves with respect to novel stimuli, apparently asking themselves, "What's that?"; they withdraw from stimuli that they do not want to continue; they remember certain stimuli previously encountered and respond positively or negatively. For these children, there is still a global workspace, it seems, albeit a highly restricted one. In the case of rats that had been surgically decorticated a few days after birth and subsequently reared by a normal mother, there was very similar behavior in search and find tasks to normal rats, as observed earlier (Panksepp et al. 1994). Patently, these rats had a working memory with a functional profile not dissimilar to that of normal rats.

5.4 Where in the Animal Realm Is Consciousness Located?

This brings me to the general question of consciousness in nonhuman animals.

If we investigate other animals and we find that their brains contain a claustrum, that is defeasible evidence that (in cases of normal development) they are indeed conscious, given the role the claustrum typically plays as a trigger for consciousness in human brains. Since all mammals have a claustrum, we thus have evidence that all mammals are conscious.

What about birds and fish? Let us take the case of birds first. Birds engage in complex and apparently purposeful behavior. For example, Caledonian crows will bend a wire into a hook to get at food located at the bottom of a narrow glass tube. Parrots can even weigh up chances to assist them in making choices (Bastos and Taylor 2020). Here is an example. Three male kea parrots were trained to associate black wooden tokens with rewards (in the form of tasty treats) and orange tokens with no reward. Two glass jars were then filled with more or less the same total number of black and orange tokens. The first jar was chock a block full of black tokens with only a few orange tokens, while the second was filled the other way around. The parrots were tested twenty times on which jar they preferred the scientists to remove a token from, and there was a clear preference for the jar with many more black tokens. In a further test, the jars both had the same number of black tokens but a different number of orange tokens. In this case, the birds showed a preference for the jar with a greater *ratio* of black to orange tokens. Since the parrots here were using the proportion of black to orange tokens in making their choices, they were weighing probabilities in making decisions, a feat previously thought to be restricted to humans and great apes.

Birds also produce songs of many kinds, which would seem entirely pointless if other birds could not hear them. Birds are also subject to visual illusions of various types, which is hard to understand if nothing appears any way to them. And they respond to pain killers as we do; they also protect and guard damaged parts of their bodies. None of this would make any real sense, if birds weren't conscious. But birds lack a neocortex. So, how is this possible?

Part of the answer is that, for the reasons already given, a cortex is not crucial for consciousness.[3] Still, it is interesting to note that there are homologous cells in bird and human brains (cells, that is, that share a common origin) that mediate the behavioral similarities. What happened with mammals was that certain sorts of cells present in non-mammalian brains and around for hundreds of millions of years were grouped together into layers to form the laminar structure of the cortex. This is what is genuinely new. But the constituent neuron types and the microcircuitry aren't new. The relevant cells for birds are preserved in a structure of a vastly different shape from the neocortex, known as the dorsal ventricular ridge (DVR). The cells in the DVR share the same physiological properties as the cortical cells (Dugas-Ford et al. 2012).

Furthermore, it has been hypothesized that within the DVR there is an homologous counterpart to the claustrum. The fact that this is the case along

---

[3] Contra Rose 2002; Key 2015.

with the fact that cells physiologically just like cortical cells are preserved in a structure that mediates complex, purposeful behavior strongly suggests that consciousness is present in birds just as it is in humans.

A physiologically similar structure of cells to the DVR is to be found in the pallium of fish (Ito and Yamamoto 2009). The pallium in birds and in fish is shown below and compared to the cortex in rodents (see Figure 7).

Furthermore, electrophysiological responses proposed to correlate with sensory binding and global broadcasting of sensory information (Baars and Franklin 2013; Crick and Koch 2003) have also been recorded from the pallium in fish. These responses include gamma frequency electrical rhythms (Prechtl et al. 1998) and sustained evoked responses to sensory stimulation (Elliot and Maler 2015). However, the question of whether a claustrum-like structure is also to be found within this brain region in fish has not been addressed yet. What are we to conclude about consciousness in fish then?

Evidence that there is global broadcasting is evidence for consciousness. Is there evidence from other sources? I suggest that there is.

Nociceptors are receptors in our skin and throughout our bodies that respond to noxious stimuli. For example, when bodily tissue is damaged or subjected to heat or pressure, nociceptors respond and send messages along nerve fibers to our brains, thereby generating the feeling of pain. Teleost fish (fish that are bony such as trout) have nociceptors too, and their nociceptors look just like ours when viewed under a microscope. This does not prove that they feel pain, of course. But they behave in response to noxious stimuli very much as we do. For example, trout have nociceptors in their lips structurally very similar to ours. When they are anaesthetized and their lips injected with bee venom or acetic acid (the main ingredient in vinegar), the trout rub their lips against the sides of the fish tank and the gravel on the bottom (once the anaesthetic wears off), and they also sit there and rock from side to side (a reaction in mammals that signifies that they are feeling or have been feeling acute discomfort).[4] In addition, teleost fish engage in trade-off behavior. This is what we do when we hold on to an extremely hot plate full of food, if we are experiencing deep hunger, even though we are experiencing pain. We trade off the pain we are feeling against our desire/need for food. Likewise, when teleost fish go to get food in an aquarium and

[4] See Sneddon 2003, 2012.

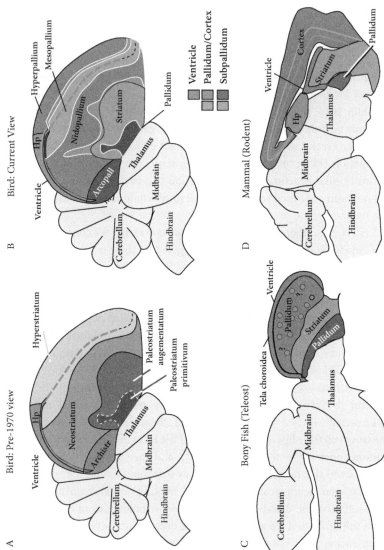

Figure 7. Bird, Bony Fish (Teleost), Mammal (Rodent).

are then electrically shocked on their flanks, afterwards they stay away from the region containing the food, but as their hunger increases, they return.[5]

There are many such examples of behavioral similarities in teleost fish and mammals in response to noxious stimuli. This is evidence that they feel pain. The inference at work here is similar effect, so similar cause—unless we have evidence that defeats this inference. This is an application of a rule formulated by Sir Isaac Newton in his Principia to the effect that we are entitled to infer like cause from like effect unless there is defeating evidence.

This rule is best seen, in my view, as providing the basis for rational preference instead of rational belief (Tye 2016), but I shall pass over that for present purposes. What is a defeater here? Well, suppose I find out that your head is empty and that you have only an organic exterior. You are really a puppet controlled remotely by Martians. This new evidence defeats my entitlement to believe the view that you have experiences and feelings like me even though you behave in very similar ways. Alternatively, suppose I find out that you have only a silicon chip in your head with a vast look-up table inscribed on it, a table that controls your every move. Again, I have a defeater. Lacking such defeaters, it is rational for me to believe that you feel pretty much what I do.

The inference goes the other way round too: same cause (reaction on nociceptors), so same effect (the feeling of pain), unless again there is defeating evidence. So, given the similar reactions on the nociceptors of fish to the reactions on our nociceptors, we have a warrant for believing that the feeling of pain is present in them as well as in us.

Do we have defeating evidence here? Given what was said earlier, we do not. The absence of a neocortex is not a defeater—witness the behavior of some decorticate children and rats; nor is the absence of a claustrum or claustrum-like physical structure (if it turns out that there is no structure homologous to the claustrum in fish brains)—witness the behavior of Damasio's patient. Nor is there neurophysiological evidence that defeats the hypothesis that there is a global workspace structure in fish brains. On the contrary, as noted earlier, there is some neurophysiological evidence in favor of global broadcasting.

---

[5] Some important research into animal consciousness focuses on meta-cognition. This is an investigation of behavior too, but more restricted behavior than I have in mind. The basic idea behind this research is that if animals behave in ways that indicate they have a cognitive grasp on how things appear to them, that is evidence they are conscious. For example, an animal that behaves in a way that indicates it recognizes how things visually appear color-wise, where the appearance is different from customary and real color of the thing, is a conscious animal.

So, a strong case can be made for the view that some fish feel pain. But do they all? Sharks lack unmyelinated nociceptors, as do other elasmobranch fish (fish that do not have a cartilaginous skeleton). But to say this is not to say that they lack nociceptors altogether. So, the immediate physiological evidence at the level of receptors is not clear.[6] As for shark behavior, again the evidence is not fully clear.[7] On the one hand, there are reports that shark do not respond as teleost fish typically do to noxious stimuli. For example, hammerhead sharks prey on stingrays. These sharks are reported to have been found with as many as ninety-six stingray barbs embedded in their mouths! There are also accounts from whale men of sharks that they have split in two continuing to feed. Likewise for sharks that have been disemboweled by other sharks attacking them. Apparently, their fatal wounds do not cause them to feel pain. Of course, it could be that there is a trade-off (as described earlier). Conceivably, in sharks, the desire to continue eating is so strong that they ignore the pain. Further, there is behavioral evidence from sharks in captivity that they experience and respond to pain. For example, in learning experiments, electric shock is aversive to sharks. Moreover, the observations of Ila France Porcher of sharks in the wild seem to support the pro-pain view.

What about simpler creatures? There is behavioral evidence that hermit crabs feel pain (Appel and Elwood 2009a, 2009b) and that honeybees feel anxiety (Bateson et al. 2011), for example.[8] So, it is rational to believe (or at least to prefer the view) that consciousness is to be found in the arthropod realm. What about direct evidence that there is a global workspace in at least some arthropods?

Bees can perform DMTS and DNMTS tasks (that is, delayed matching to sample and delayed non-matching to sample tasks) and use their solutions to find their way to rewards. Moreover, they can do this using both colors and odors. For example, if bees are shown a blue disk at the entrance to a maze made up of Y-shaped tubes, they can learn to take the blue colored exit tube in each Y-tube, thereby finding their way to a reward (a DMTS task). Where one exit tube for each Y is painted blue and the other painted green, they can also learn to take the tube with the *opposite* color to the blue disk at the entrance (the sample). This is a DNMTS task. These tasks require that

---

[6] I am indebted here to George Bates.

[7] To be sure, sharks caught on fishing lines struggle to get away as do other fish. But this seems no more than a reflex: the line interferes with their free movement and so they reflexively try to free themselves.

[8] Also, there is not just behavioral evidence, but neurochemical evidence too.

the bees use information in working memory to reason and make decisions. Using the information in memory to respond cognitively in these ways is a matter of the information being available in a workspace and playing a certain functional role—a role of the sort postulated in global workspace theory. There is also an extraordinary variety in bee behavior based on sensory information. For example, bees use landmarks and celestial cues (such as the position of the sun) to navigate. They gather food by visiting hundreds of flowers one after another; they check out places for potential nests; they exchange information with one another about food and nest sites via "waggle dances". They can identify orientations of items as such and respond to those orientations when present in new cases. For example, they can be trained to distinguish between horizontal and vertical black and white stripes and to transfer this distinction to things other than stripes. They see the world in color;[9] their olfactory sense is acute.

According to Menzel and Giurfa (2001), the overall complexity of bee behavior is such that it cannot be explained simply by independent, domain-specific modules of the sort associated in philosophy with Jerry Fodor (1983). There are such sensory-motor modules in the honeybee, but they need to be integrated into a central state, and representations in that central state then drive reasoning, decision making, and behavior. If this is correct and there is indeed in bees a central integration state of this sort, there seem to be all the ingredients in place for global broadcasting. Evidence that this is the case is evidence for the hypothesis that there is a global workspace and thus that consciousness is present in bees.

It is interesting to note that insect brains generally have a shared ana-tomical plan. Vision and smell are processed in dedicated sensory lobes and sensory representations are generated there. The central complex of the insect brain processes this information from different senses and uses it so that the insect can orient and navigate. This is no simple matter. Think about the case of a tourist using visual landmarks to orient herself and navigate to a particular target. The coordination needed between the senses and bodily movements is highly complex and the decision making involved in picking a route can take into account not only present information but also past experience, for example, knowledge that a particular route is crammed with other tourists and is best avoided.

---

[9] Von Frisch 1915.

Adaptive sensory motor coupling of this sort is the responsibility of the central complex in insects. For example, in Monarch butterflies and locusts the central complex handles sun-compass navigation; in fruit flies, it handles visual landmark position and orientation; in cockroaches, it controls antenna-guided obstacle navigation. In insects generally, then, the central complex is responsible for integrating information and using it cognitively to drive decisions and behavior (Turner-Evans et al. 2016). The evidence that this is the case is evidence for global broadcasting, and with it evidence for consciousness across the insect realm. What is variable is the richness of the consciousness. Honey bees are at the top end of the spectrum and termites are at the other.

In the case of insect pain, as with sharks, the situation is not fully clear. Unlike mammals, many insects do not show protective behavior with respect to parts of their bodies that have been injured. They do not limp if they injure their legs, nor do they stop feeding or mating even if their bodies are severely damaged. Locusts have been observed to continue to feed while themselves being eaten by mantises; tse-tse flies that have been half-dissected do not stop feeding; male mantids that are mating continue to mate even as they are being eaten by their partners (Eisemann et al. 1984). These observations support the view that insects do not feel pain.

There is evidence that goes the other way, however. Fruit flies placed in a glass tube in which there is a light gradient move towards the light. But if the center of the tube is heated, they are inhibited from going through it towards the light. Specific analgesics (agonists for $GABA_b$) diminish this inhibition, and the flies pass through the heated part (Dimitrijevic et al. 2005). These agonists are effective as analgesics in hot-plate tests on rats (Britto et al. 2012). The suggestion that fruit flies feel pain also fits well with the claims made by Neely et al. (2010) about striking commonalities in gene pathways in fruit flies and mice, pathways that aid mice in sensing pain and fixing pain thresholds. If they do this in mice, why not also in flies? It turns out that there are 580 genes in these pathways in flies and 400 in mammals. The general suggestion made by Neely is that the gene networks are similar not only in flies and mice but also in other species and that this conservation of genes across species is what underwrites the ability to feel pain—an ability that prima facie is important to any animal's survival.

Also, according to a recent study (Neely et al. 2019), there is evidence that fruit flies can feel chronic pain. In a series of tests, fruit flies had legs amputated in a laboratory. After the wounds had time to heal, the flies were exposed to a hot room. It was found that the flies tried to escape the room at much lower temperatures than before they had a leg amputated. Apparently, the flies, like other animals, are hyper-sensitized to possible sources of new pain after being previously injured. In other animals with a spinal cord what happens in such cases is that the injured nerve no longer blocks or moderates the responses of inhibitory neurons (that is, neurons with responses that inhibit pain) in the spinal cord with the result that the pain threshold changes and the animals become hyper-vigilant. In place of a spinal cord, fruit flies have a ventral nerve cord and something similar seems to be going on in the fruit flies' nerve cord after nerve injury.

Whatever is the truth about pain in the insect realm, once we acknowledge that consciousness is present in insects generally, it may be tempting to suppose that *wherever* there is a brain in the invertebrate realm, there is consciousness. This would be too fast, however. Consider the case of the cubozoan box jellyfish *Tripedalia cystophora*. This species has twenty-four lensed eyes distributed around the body and it engages in active hunting of its prey. But there is no central control system and no global broadcasting. Here is how Barron and Klein (2016, p. 4904) describe this jellyfish:

> Sense organs independently modulate activity in regions of the sensory net and muscle walls to steer the animal. The outcome of local sensory input acting on local muscle activity is an adaptive change in the swimming direction and speed of the animal, but the simple behavioral control system is entirely decentralized. Although such systems manifest the appearance of adaptive and dynamic targeting, they are nothing more than simple decentralized stimulus–response systems.

The conclusion to draw is that the box jellyfish lacks consciousness.

The same is true for the leech. Leeches have segmented bodies and a brain that is distributed through the different segments. Each segment has its own neurons (around 400) and these neurons are connected to the neurons in adjacent segments. Leeches are very responsive to light and mechanical stimuli. But as with the box jellyfish, their behavior is the product of decentralized stimulus response systems. There is no decision making as such. For example, leeches do not decide to go to where food is *expected* to be on the basis of past experience. They simply detect their prey using chemo- and mechano-reception. For example, bloodsucking leeches respond to vibrations via mechanoreceptors and then, after following the vibrations, they focus on their prey via chemoreceptors that track scent. As with the box jellyfish, there is no consciousness.

The table below summarizes some of the central claims of this chapter.

	Consciousness	Prefrontal Cortex Activity
Normal humans	Yes	Yes
Human: claustrum destroyed	Yes	Yes
Human: claustrum electrically stimulated	No	No (in relevant areas)
(Some) decorticate children	Yes	No
Rats: cortex removed at birth	Yes	No
Birds and fish	Yes	No
Honeybees	Yes	No
Box jellyfish	No	No
Leeches	No	No

Bibliography

Aaronson, S. 2014. "Why I am not an Integrated Information Theorist," https://www.scottaaronson.com/blog/?p=1799.

Alter, T. and Pereboom, D. 2019. "Russellian Monism," entry in *Stanford Encyclopedia of Philosophy*, online.

Antony, M. 2006. "Vagueness and the Metaphysics of Consciousness," *Philosophical Studies* 128, pp. 515–38.

Appel, M. and Elwood, R. W. 2009a. "Gender Differences, Responsiveness and Memory of a Potentially Painful Event in Hermit Crabs," *Animal Behavior* 78, pp. 1373–9.

Appel, M. and Elwood, R. W. 2009b. "Motivational Trade-Offs and the Potential for Pain Experience in Hermit Crabs," *Applied Animal Behaviour Science* 119, pp. 120–4.

Armstrong, D. 1962. *Bodily Sensations*, London: Routledge and Kegan Paul.

Baars, B. 1988. *A Cognitive Theory of Consciousness*, New York: Cambridge University Press.

Baars, B. and Franklin, S. 2013. "Global Workspace Dynamics: Cortical 'Binding and Propagation' Enables Conscious Contents," *Frontiers in Psychology*, 4.

Baddeley, A. D. 2000. "The Episodic Buffer: A New Component of Working Memory?" *Trends in Cognitive Sciences* 4, pp. 417–23.

Baddeley, A. D. and Hitch, G. J. 1974. "Working Memory," in *The Psychology of Learning and Motivation*, ed. Bower, pp. 47–89, Academic Press.

Barron, A. and Klein. 2016. "What Insects Can Tell Us about the Origins of Consciousness," *Proceedings of the National Academy of Sciences USA* 113, pp. 4900–8.

Bastos, A. P. M. and Taylor, A. H. 2020. "Kea Show Three Signatures of Domain-general Statistical Inference," *Nature Communications* 11, p. 828. https://doi.org/10.1038/s41467-020-14695-1.

Bateson, M., Desire, S., Gartside, S., and Wright, G. 2011. "Agitated Honeybees Exhibit Pessimistic Cognitive Biases," *Current Biology* 21(12), pp. 1070–3.

Benchley, R. 1921. *Inside Benchley*, New York: Harper and Bros.

Block, N. 1981. "Psychologism and Behaviorism," *Philosophical Review* 90, pp. 5–43.

Block, N. 1990. "Inverted Earth," in J. Tomberlin (ed.), *Philosophical Perspectives* 4, Ridgeview, pp. 52–79. Reprinted in Block et al. (eds.) 1997. *The Nature of Consciousness: Philosophical Debates*, Cambridge, Mass: MIT Press.

Block, N. 1998. "On a Confusion about a Function of Consciousness," in *The Nature of Consciousness*, ed. N. Block, O. Flanagan, and G. Guzeldere, , pp. 375–415. Cambridge, Mass: The MIT Press.

Block, N. 2001. "Mental Paint," in M. Hahn and B. Ramberg (eds.), *Essays in Honor of Tyler Burge*, Cambridge, Mass: MIT Press.

Block, N. 2006. "Bodily Sensations as an Obstacle for Representationalism," in *Pain: New Essays on its Nature and the Methodology of its Study*, ed. M. Aydede, Cambridge, Mass: The MIT Press, pp. 137–42.

Boghossian, P. and Velleman, D. 1989. "Colour as a Secondary Quality," *Mind* 98, pp. 89–103.

Braddon-Mitchell, D. and Jackson, F. 1996. *Philosophy of Mind and Cognition*, Oxford: Blackwells.

Bradley, P. and Tye, M. 2001. "Of Colors, Kestrels, Caterpillars, and Leaves," *Journal of Philosophy* 98, pp. 469–87.

Breitmeyer, B. and Ogmen, H. 2000. "Recent Models and Findings in Visual Backward Masking: A Comparison, Review, and Update," *Perceptual Psychophysics* 62, pp. 1572–95.

Britto, G., Subash, K., Rao, J., Varghese, B., and Kumar, S. 2012. "A Synergistic Approach to Evaluate the Anti-Nociceptive Activity of a GABA Agonist with Opioids in Albino Mice," *Journal of Clinical and Diagnostic Research* 6, pp. 682–7.

Byrne, A. 2012. "Hmm . . . Hill on the Paradox of Pain," *Philosophical Studies* 161, pp. 489–96.

Cannon, W. 1929. *Bodily Changes in Pain, Hunger, Fear and Rage*, 2nd Ed. New York: Appleton.

Chalmers, D. 1995. "Facing Up to the Problem of Consciousness," *Journal of Consciousness Studies* 2, pp. 200–19.

Chalmers, D. 1995. *The Conscious Mind*, Oxford: Oxford University Press.

Chalmers, D. 1997. "Moving Forward on the Problem of Consciousness," *Journal of Consciousness Studies* 4(1), pp. 3–46.

Chalmers, D. 2002. "Consciousness and its Place in Nature," in *Philosophy of Mind, Classical and Contemporary Readings*, ed. D. Chalmers, Oxford: Oxford University Press, pp. 247–272.

Chalmers, D. 2012. *Constructing the World*, Oxford: Oxford University Press.

Chalmers, D. forthcoming. "The Combination Problem for Panpsychism," in *Panpsychism*, ed. G. Bruntrup and L. Jaskolla. Oxford: Oxford University Press.

Chibeni, S. 2006. "Ontic Vagueness in Microphysics," http://www.sorites.org 15, pp. 29–41.

Coleman, S. 2014. "The Real Combination Problem: Panpsychism, Micro-subjects, and Emergence," *Erkenntnis* 79(1), pp. 19–44.

Cox, J. F. 2005. "In the Matter of Terri Schiavo: Some Science and Ethics," *Postcards from Winticomack*, http://www.winticomack.com/article.php?essay=a051231.

Crane, T. 2006. "Is There a Perceptual Relation?" in *Perceptual Experience*, ed. T. Gendler and J. Hawthorne, Oxford: Oxford University Press, pp. 126–146.

Crick, F. and Koch, C. 1990. "Towards a Neurobiological Theory of Consciousness," *Seminars in the Neurosciences* 2, pp. 263–75.

Crick, F. and Koch, C. 2003. "A Framework for Consciousness," *Nature Neuroscoence* 6, pp. 119–26.

Crick, F. and Koch, C. 2005. "What is the Function of the Claustrum?" *Philosophical Transactions* B, The Royal Society 360, pp. 1271–9.

Damasio, A. 2013. "The Nature of Feelings: Evolutionary and Neurobiological Origins," *Nature Reviews Neuroscience* 14, pp. 143–52.

Dennett, D. 1973. "Mechanism and Responsibility," in *Essays on Freedom of Action*, ed. T. Honderich, London: Routledge and Kegan Paul. Page references to reprint in *Brainstorms*, Cambridge, MA: The MIT Press, pp. 233–55.

Dennett D. 2004. "Determinants of Emotional States," *Psychological Review* 69, pp. 379–99.

Dimitrijevic, N., Dzitoyeva, S., Satta, R., Imbesi, M., Yildiz, S., and Manev, H. 2005. "Drosophila GABA(B) Receptors Are Involved in Behavioral Effects of Gamma-Hydroxybutyric Acid (GHB)," *European Journal of Pharmacology* 519(3), pp. 246–52.

Dretske, F. 1988. *Explaining Behavior*, Cambridge, MA: The MIT Press.

Dretske, F. 1993. "Conscious Experience," *Mind* 102, pp. 263–83.

Dretske, F. 1995. *Naturalizing the Mind*, Cambridge, MA: The MIT Press.

Dretske, F. 1999. "The Mind's Awareness of Itself," *Philosophical Studies* 95, pp. 103–24.

Dugas-Ford, J., Rowell, J., and Ragsdale, C. 2012. "Cell-Type Homologies and the Origins of the Neocortex," *Proceedings of the National Academy of Sciences* 109, pp. 16974–9.

Eisemann, C. H., Jorgensen, W. K., Merritt, D. J., Rice, M. J., Cribb, B. W., Webb, P. D., and Zalucki, M. P. 1984. "Do Insects Feel Pain? A Biological View," *Experientia* 40, pp. 164–7.

Elliott, S. and Maler, L. 2015. "Stimulus-induced Up States in the Dorsal Pallium of a Weakly Electric Fish," *Journal of Neurophysiology* 114, pp. 2071–6.

Elwood, R. W. and Appel, M. 2009. "Pain Experience in Hermit Crabs?" *Animal Behaviour* 77, pp. 1243–6.

Feigl, H. 1967. *The Mental and the Physical*, University of Minnesota Press, Minneapolis.

Field, H. 1994. "Disquotational Truth and Factually Defective Discourse," *Philosophical Review* 103, pp. 405–52.

Fine, K. 1999. "Things and their Parts," *Midwest Studies in Philosophy* 23(1), pp. 61–74.

Fine, K. 2003. "The Non-identity of a Material Thing and its Matter," *Mind* 112, pp. 195–234.

Fine, K. 2006. "Arguing for Nonidentity: A Reply to King and Frances," *Mind*, 115, pp.187–210.

Fine, K. 2012. "Guide to Ground," in F. Correia and B. Schnieder (eds.), *Metaphysical Grounding*, Cambridge: Cambridge University Press, pp. 37–80.

Fodor, J. 1983. *The Modularity of Mind*, Cambridge, Mass: The MIT Press.

Fodor, J. 1987. *Psychosemantics*, Cambridge, Mass: The MIT Press.

Frances, B. 2006. "The New Leibniz's Law Arguments for Pluralism," *Mind* 115, pp. 1007–22.

Goff, P. 2006. "Experiences Don't Sum," in *Consciousness and Its Place in Nature*, ed. A. Freeman, pp. 53–61. Exeter: Imprint Academic.

Goff, P. 2009. "Why Panpsychism Doesn't Help Us Explain Consciousness," *Dialectica* 63(3), pp. 289–311.

Harman, G. 1990. "The Intrinsic Quality of Experience," *Philosophy of Mind and Action Theory: Philosophical Perspectives* 4, pp. 31–52.

Hawthorne, J. and Kovakovitch, K. 2006. "Disjunctivism," *Proceedings of the Aristotelian Society, Supplementary Volume* 80, pp. 145–83.

Heck, R. 2000. "Nonconceptual Content and the 'Space of Reasons'," *Philosophical Review* 109, pp. 483–523.

Ito, H. and Yamamoto, N. 2009. "Non-laminar Cerebral Cortex in Teleost Fish?" *Biological Letters* 5, pp. 117–21.

James, W. 1890. *The Principles of Psychology*, Vols. 1 and 2, New York: Dover Publications.

James, W. 1884. "What is an Emotion?" *Mind* 19, pp. 188–204.

Johnston, M. 2004. "The Obscure Object of Hallucination," *Philosophical Studies* 120, pp. 113–83.

Kant, I. [1785] 1998. *Groundwork of the Metaphysics of Morals (Grundlegung zur Metaphysik der Sitten)*, M. J. Gregor (trans.), Cambridge: Cambridge University Press.

Kant, I. [1798] 2010. "Anthropology from a Pragmatic Point of View (1798)," in *Anthropology, History, and Education* (Cambridge Edition of the Works of Immanuel Kant), Robert Louden and Gunter Zoller (eds. and trans.), pp. 227–429. Cambridge: Cambridge University Press.

Kennedy, M. 2009. "Heirs of Nothing: The Implications of Transparency," *Philosophy and Phenomenological Research* 79, pp. 574–604.

Key, B. 2015. "Why Fish (Likely) Don't Feel Pain," *Scientia Salon* (blog), scientiasalon.wordpress.com/2015/02/05/why- fish- likely- don't- feel- pain.

Kind, A. 2003. "What's So Transparent about Transparency?" *Philosophical Studies* 115, pp. 225–44.

Kind, A. 2013. "The Case Against Representationalism about Moods," in *Current Controversies in the Philosophy of Mind*, ed. U. Kriegel, Routledge.

Kind, A. forthcoming. "Pessimism about Russellian Monism," in *Consciousness in the Physical World: Essays on Russellian Monism*, ed. T. Alter and Y. Nagasawa, Oxford: Oxford University Press.

King, J. C. 2006. "Semantics for Monists," *Mind* 115, pp. 1024–58.

Kobeissi, M. et al. 2014. "Electrical Stimulation of a Small Brain Area Reversibly Disrupts Consciousness," *Epilepsy Behavior* 37, pp. 32–5.

Koch, C. 2008. "Exploring Consciousness through the Study of Bees," *Scientific American Mind* 19.6, pp. 18–19.

Kosslyn, S. 1994. *Image and Brain: The Resolution of the Imagery Debate*. Cambridge, Mass: The MIT Press.

Kosslyn, S. M., Thompson, W. L., Kim, I. J., and Alpert, N. M. 1995. "Topographic Representations of Mental Images in Primary Visual Cortex," *Nature* 378(6556), pp. 496–8.

LeDoux, J. 1996. *The Emotional Brain*, New York: Simon and Schuster; Oxford University Press.

Levin, J. 2019. "Representational Exhaustion," in *Blockheads*, ed. D. Stoljar and A. Pautz, pp. 247–72. Cambridge, Masss: The MIT Press.

Levine, J. 1983. "Materialism and Qualia: The Explanatory Gap," *Pacific Philosophical Quarterly* 64, pp. 354–61.

Lewis, D. 1973. *Counterfactuals*, Oxford: Blackwells.

Lewis, D. 2000. "Causation as Influence," *Journal of Philosophy* 97, pp. 182–97.

Lewtas, P. 2013. "What It is Like to Be a Quark," *Journal of Consciousness Studies* 20 (9–10), pp. 39–64.

Loar, B. 2003. "Transparent Experience and the Availability of Qualia," in *Consciousness: New Philosophical Essays*, ed. A. Jokic and Q. Smith, Oxford: Oxford University Press.

Lycan W. 1996. *Consciousness*, Cambridge, Mass: The MIT Press.

Marcel, A. 1998. "Blindsight and Shape Perception: Deficit of Visual Consciousness or of Visual Function?" *Brain* 121, pp. 1565–15.

Marti, S., Sigman, M., and Dehaene, S. 2012. "A Shared Cortical Bottleneck Underlying Attentional Blink and Psychological Refractory Period: Central and Sensory Processing in Dual-tasks," *Neuro-Image*, Elsevier 59, pp. 2883–98.

Martin, M. 2002. "The Transparency of Experience," *Mind and Language* 4(4), pp. 376–425.

Maxwell, G. 1978. "Rigid Designators and Mind-Brain Identity," *Minnesota Studies in the Philosophy of Science* 9, pp. 395–403.

McGinn C. 1982. *The Character of Mind*, Oxford: Oxford University Press.

Mendelovici, A. 2013. "Pure Intentionalism about Moods and Emotions," in *Current Controversies in the Philosophy of Mind*, ed. U. Kriegel, Routledge.

Menzel, R. and Giurfa, M. 2001. "Cognitive Architecture of a Mini-Brain: The Honeybee," *Trends in Cognitive Sciences* 5, pp. 62–71.

Merker, B. 2005. "The Liabilities of Mobility: A Selection Pressure for the Transition to Consciousness in Animal Evolution," *Conscious Cognition* 14, pp. 89–114.

Merker, B. 2007. "Consciousness Without a Cerebral Cortex: A Challenge for Neuroscience and Medicine," with commentaries, in *The Behavioral and Brain Sciences* 30, pp. 63–134.

Montero, B. 2010. "A Russellian Response to the Structural Argument against Physicalism," *Journal of Consciousness Studies* 17, pp. 3–4.

Moore, G. E. 1903. "The Refutation of Idealism," *Mind* 12, pp. 433–53.

Neely, G., Hess, M. Costigan, M., et al. 2010. "A Genome-Wide Drosophila Screen for Heat Nociception Identifies $\alpha 2\delta 3$ as an Evolutionarily Conserved Pain Gene," *Cell* 143(4), pp. 628–38.

Neely, G., Khuong, T., Wang, Q., Manion, J., Oyston, L., Lau, M., Towler, H., and Lin, Y. 2019. "Nerve Injury Drives a Heightened State of Vigilance and Neuropathic Sensitization," *Drosophila, Science Advances* 10.

Nida-Rumelin, M. 2007. "Transparency of Experience and the Perceptual Model of Phenomenal Awareness," *Philosophical Perspectives* 1, pp. 429–55.

Nikolajsen, N. and Jensen, T. 2001. "Phantom Limb Pain," *Journal of Anaethesiology* 87, pp. 107–16.

Palmer, S. and Schloss, K. 2010. "An Ecological Valence Theory of Human Color Preference," *Proceedings of the National Academy of Sciences of the United States of America* 107, pp. 8877–88.

Panksepp, J. 1998. *Series in Affective Science. Affective Neuroscience: The Foundations of Human and Animal Emotions*, New York, NY: Oxford University Press.

Panksepp, J., Normansell, L., Cox, J., and Siviy, S. 1994 "Effects of Neonatal Decortication on the Social Play of Juvenile Rats," *Physiology and Behavior* 56, pp. 429–43.

Papineau, D. 1993. *Philosophical Naturalism*, Oxford: Blackwells.

Papineau, D. 2002. *Thinking About Consciousness*, Oxford: Oxford University Press.

Pashler, H. 1998. *Attention*, Psychology Press.

Pautz, A. 2007. "Intentionalism and Perceptual Presence," *Philosophical Perspectives* 21 (Philosophy of Mind), ed. John Hawthorne. Malden, MA, Blackwell, pp. 495–541.

Pautz, A. 2019. "What is the Integrated Information Theory of Consciousness," *Journal of Consciousness Studies* 1, pp. 1–2.

Pautz, A. 2020. "Representationalism about Consciousness," in *Oxford Handbook of the Philosophy of Consciousness*, ed. U. Kriegel, Oxford University Press, Oxford.

Pautz, A. forthcoming. "A Dilemma for Russellian Monists about Consciousness."

Peacocke, C. 1983. *Sense and Content*. Oxford: Oxford University Press.

Prechtl, J. C., von der Emde, G., Wolfart, J., Karamürsel, S., Akoev, G. N., Andrianov, Y. N., and Bullock, T. H. 1998. "Sensory Processing in the Pallium of a Mormyrid Fish," *Journal of Neuroscience* 18, pp. 7381–93.

Queller, D. and Strassman, J. 2009. "Beyond Society: The Evolution of Organismality," *Philosophical Transactions of the Royal Society London B Biological Sciences* 364, pp. 3143–55.

Raymond, J., Shapiro, K., and Arnell, K. 1992. "Temporary Suppression of Visual Processing in an RSVP Task: An Attentional Blink?" *Journal of Experimental Psychology, Human Perception and Performance* 18, pp. 849–60.

Roelofs, L. 2019. *Combining Minds*, Oxford: Oxford University Press.

Rose, J. D. 2002. "The Neurobehavioral Nature of Fishes and the Question of Awareness of Pain," *Reviews in Fisheries Sciences* 10(1), pp. 1–38.

Rose, J. D., Arlinghaus, R., Cooke, S. J., Diggles, B. K., Sawynok, W., Stevens, E. D., and Wynne, C. D. L. 2014. "Can Fish Really Feel Pain?" *Fish and Fisheries* 15, pp. 97–133.

Russell, B. 1927. *The Analysis of Matter*, London: Kegan Paul.

Sainsbury, M. and Tye, M. 2011. *Seven Puzzles of Thought*, Oxford: Oxford University Press.

Schacter, S. and Singer, J. 1962. "Cognitive, Social and Physiological Determinants of Emotional State," *Psychological Review* 69, pp. 379–99.

Seager, W. 2002. "Emotional Introspection," *Conscious Cognition* 11, pp. 666–87.

Seager, W. 2006. "The 'Intrinsic Nature' Argument for Panpsychism," *Journal of Consciousness Studies* 13, pp. 129–45.

Seager, W. Forthcoming. "Panpsychism, Aggregation and Combinatorial Infusion," In *Panpsychism*, ed. G. Bruntrup and L. Jaskolla. Oxford: Oxford University Press.

Searle J. 1992. *The Rediscovery of Mind*, Cambridge, Mass: The MIT Press.

Searle, J. 1983. *Intentionality: An Essay in the Philosophy of Mind*, Cambridge: Cambridge University Press.

Sellars, W. 1963. *Science, Perception and Reality*, London: Routledge & Kegan Paul Ltd; New York: The Humanities Press.

Shewmon, A., Holmes, G., and Byrne, P. 1999. "Consciousness in Congenitally Decorticate Children: 'Developmental Vegetative State' as Self-Fulfilling Prophecy," *Developmental Medicine and Child Neurology*, pp. 364–74.

Shoemaker, S. 1994. 'Phenomenal Character', *Nous* 28, pp. 21–38.

Siewert, C. 2004. "Is Experience Transparent?" *Philosophical Studies* 117, pp. 15–41.

Simon, J. 2017. "Vagueness and Zombies: Why 'Phenomenally Conscious' has No Borderline Cases," *Philosophical Studies* 174, pp. 2105–23.

Smart J. J. C. 1959. "Sensations and Brain Processes," *Philosophical Review* 68, pp. 141–56.

Smith, A. O. 2008. "Translucent Experiences," *Philosophical Studies* 140, pp. 197–212.

Sneddon, L. 2003. "The Evidence for Pain in Fish: The Use of Morphine as an Analgesic," *Applied Animal Behaviour Science* 83(2), pp. 153–62.

Sneddon, L. 2012. "Pain Perception in Fish: Evidence and Implications for the Use of Fish," *Journal of Consciousness Studies* 18, pp. 209–29.

Speaks, J. 2009. "Transparency, Intentionalism, and the Nature of Perceptual Content," *Philosophy and Phenomenological Research* 79, pp. 539–73.

Stoljar, D. 2001. "Two Conceptions of the Physical," *Philosophy and Phenomenological Research* 62, pp. 253–81.

Stoljar, D. 2004. "The Argument from Diaphanousness," in *New Essays in the Philosophy of Language and Mind*, ed. M. Ezcurdia, R. J. Stainton, and C. Viger, Calgary: Calgary University Press.

Stoljar, D. 2006. "Comments on Galen Strawson: 'Realistic Monism: Why Physicalism entails Panpsychism',' *Journal of Consciousness Studies* 13, p. 170.

Strawson, G. 2006. "Realistic Monism: Why Physicalism Entails Panpsychism," *Journal of Consciousness Studies* 13, pp. 3–31.

Tononi, G. Boly, M. Massimini, M., and Koch, C. 2016. "Integrated Information Theory: From Consciousness to its Physical Substrate," *Nature Reviews Neuroscience* 17, pp. 450–61.

Turner-Evans, D. and Jayaraman, V. 2016. "The Insect Central Complex," *Current Biology* 6, pp. R453–7.

Tye, M. 1996. "Is Consciousness Vague or Arbitrary?", *Philosophy and Phenomenological Research* 56, pp. 679–85.

Tye, M. 1992. "Visual Qualia and Visual Content" in T. Crane (ed.), *The Contents of Experience*, pp. 158–76. Cambridge: Cambridge University Press.

Tye, M. 1995. "A Representational Theory of Pains and their Phenomenal Character," in *Philosophical Perspectives*, ed. by J. Tomberlin, Vol. 9; reprinted in *Essays on Consciousness: Philosophical and Scientific Debates*, ed. N. Block,

O. Flanagan, and G. Guzeldere, Cambridge, Mass: The MIT Press; Bradford Books (1996).

Tye, M. 1995. *Ten Problems of Consciousness*, Cambridge, Mass: The MIT Press.

Tye, M. 2000. *Consciousness, Color, and Content*, Cambridge, Mass: Bradford Books; the MIT Press.

Tye, M. (with P. Bradley). 2001. "Of Colors, Kestrels, Caterpillars, and Leaves," *Journal of Philosophy* 98, pp. 469–87.

Tye, M. 2003. "Blurry Images, Double Vision, and Other Oddities: New Problems for Representationalism?" in Q. Smith and A. Jokic (eds.), *Consciousness: New Philosophical Perspectives*, Oxford: Oxford University Press.

Tye, M. 2003. *Consciousness and Persons*, Cambridge, Mass: The MIT Press.

Tye, M. 2005. "Another Look at Representationalism about Pain," in *Pain*, ed. M. Aydede, Cambridge, Mass: The MIT Press.

Tye, M. 2006a. "Nonconceptual Content, Richness, and Fineness of Grain," in *Perceptual Experience*, ed. T. Gendler and J. Hawthorne, Oxford: Oxford University Press.

Tye, M. 2006b. "In Defense of Representationalism: Reply to Commentaries," in *Pain: New Essays on its Nature and the Methodology of its Study*, ed. M. Aydede, Cambridge, Mass: The MIT Press.

Tye, M. 2008. "The Experience of Emotion: An Intentionalist Theory," *Revue Internationale de Philosophie*, special volume on philosophy of mind, edited by Joelle Proust.

Tye, M. 2009. *Consciousness Revisited*, Cambridge, Mass: The MIT Press.

Tye, M. 2010. "Attention, Seeing and Change Blindness," *Philosophical Issues* 10, pp. 410–37.

Tye, M. (with B. Wright). 2010. "Is There a Phenomenology of Thought?", in *The Unity of Consciousness*, ed. T. Bayne, Oxford: Oxford University Press.

Tye, M. (with B. Cutter). 2011. "Tracking Representationalism and the Painfulness of Pain," *Philosophical Issues* 21, pp. 90–109.

Tye, M. 2014. "Transparency, Qualia Realism and Representationalism," *Philosophical Studies* 170, pp. 39–57.

Tye, M. 2015. "Yes, Phenomenal Character Really is Out There in the World," *Philosophy and Phenomenological Research* 91, pp. 483–8.

Tye, M. 2016. "The Nature of Pain and the Appearance/Reality Distinction," in *The Nature of Phenomenal Qualities*, ed. P. Coates, Oxford: Oxford University Press.

Tye, M. 2016. *Tense Bees and Shell-Shocked Crabs: Are Animals Conscious?*, Oxford: Oxford University Press.

Tye, M. 2017. "Are Pains Feelings?" *The Monist* 100, pp. 478–84.

Tye, M. 2017. "How to Think about the Representational Content of Visual Experience," in Proceedings of the 40th International Ludwig Wittgenstein symposium in Kirchberg, Austria, 2016, *The Philosophy of Perception and Observation*, edited by Christoph Limbeck, De Gruyer.

Tye, M. 2019. "Homunculi Head and Silicon Chips: The Importance of History to Phenomenology," in *Themes from Block*, ed. A. Pautz and D. Stoljar, Cambridge, Mass: MIT Press.

Tye, M. forthcoming. "What Uninformed Mary Can Tell Us," in a collection of essays edited by S. Coleman, Cambridge: Cambridge University Press.

Van Gaal S., De Lange F. P., and Cohen M. X. 2012. "The Role of Consciousness in Cognitive Control and Decision Making," *Frontiers in Human Neuroscience* 6, p. 121.

Van Gulick, R. 1993. "Understanding the Phenomenal Mind: Are We all just Armadillos?" in M. Davies and G. Humphreys (eds.), *Consciousness*, pp. 137–54. Oxford: Basil Blackwell.

Von Frisch, K. 1915. *"Der Farben-und Formensinn der Bienen,"* *Zoologische Jahrbücher (Physiologie)* 35, pp. 1–188.

Watkins, S. and Rees, G. 2007. "The Human Superior Colliculus: Neither Necessary nor Sufficient for Consciousness?" *Behavioral and Brain Sciences* 30, p. 108.

Weiskrantz L. 1988. "Some Contributions of Neuropsychology of Vision and Memory to the Problem of Consciousness," in A. J. Marcel and E. Bisiach (eds.), *Consciousness in Contemporary Science*, pp. 183–99. Oxford: Clarendon Press.

White, A. 1964. *Attention*, Oxford: Blackwell. Wiley-Blackwell.

Williamson, T. 1994. *Vagueness*, London: Routledge.

Wright, C. 2003. "Vagueness: A Fifth Column Approach," in J. C. Beall and M. Glanzberg (eds.), *Liars & Heaps: New Essays on Paradox*, pp. 84–105. Oxford: Oxford University Press.

Yablo, S. 1992. "Mental Causation," *Philosophical Review "* 101, pp. 245–80.

Yamamoto, N. 2009. "Studies on the Teleost Brain Morphology in Search of the Origin of Cognition," *Japanese Psychological Research* 51, pp. 154–67.

Index of Names

For the benefit of digital users, indexed terms that span two pages (e.g., 52–53) may, on occasion, appear on only one of those pages.

Aaronson, S. 8–9
Alter, Torin 23
Antony, M. 5n.1, 16–17
Appel, M. 112
Armstrong, D. 44

Baars, B. 87, 109
Barron, A. 115
Bastos, A. P. M. 107–8
Bateson, M. 112
Block, N. 27n.5, 34, 45n.8, 62–4, 83n.7, 86
Boghossian, P. 63–4
Bradley, P. 91n.14
Breitmeyer, B. 87
Brentano, F. 65
Burge, T. 16n.7
Byrne, A. 45
Byrne, P. 106

Cannon, W. 48–9
Chalmers, D. 23–6, 91
Chibeni, S. 11–12n.4
Coleman, S. 27n.3
Cox, J. F. 104
Crane, T. 41–2
Crick, F. 6–7, 100–3, 109

Damasio, A. 102–3, 105–6, 111
Dennett, D. 4–5, 83
Descartes, R. 25–6
Dimitrijevic, N. 114
Dretske, F. 34–5, 56, 90–1, 94–6
Dugas-Ford, J. 108

Elliott, S. 109
Elwood, R. W. 112

Feigl, H. 4, 12
Fine, K. 9, 29–30, 66, 95n.15

Fodor, J. 78–9, 113
Franklin, S. 109

Gingrass, G. 104
Giurfa, M. 113
Goff, P. 27n.3

Harman, G. 32–3, 62–3, 69
Hawthorne, J. 65
Holmes, G. 106

Ito, H. 109

Jackson, F. 66, 83n.7
James, W. 48–50
Jensen, T. 45
Johnston, M. 58, 66, 70n.25

Kant, I. 91–2
Kennedy, M. 64–5, 67
Kind, A. 20n.1, 54–5, 67–8
Klein, C. 115
Kobeissi, M. 100–3, 105–6
Koch, C. 6–7, 100–3, 109
Kovakovitch, K. 65

LeDoux, J. 49–50
Le Verrier, Urbain J. J. 75
Levin, J. 42
Lewis, D. 98n.16
Lewtas, P. 27–8
Loar, B. 67n.24
Lycan, W. 4–5

Maler, L. 109
Martin, M. 64
Marti, S. 94
Maxwell, G. 24
McGinn, C. 5–6
Meinong, A. 65

Mendelovici, A. 54–5
Menzel, R. 113
Merker, B. 103–4, 106
Montero, B. 24
Moore, G. E. 31–2, 62, 71–2, 76–7

Neely, G. 114–15
Newton, I. 111
Nida-Rumelin, M. 68–9
Nikolajsen, N. 45

Ogmen, H. 87

Palmer, S. 47–8
Panksepp, J. 103, 107
Papineau, D. 5, 13
Paré, A. 45–6
Pashler, H. 37n.4
Pautz, A. 9, 26n.2, 61n.21, 66
Peacocke, C. 63–4
Pereboom, D. 23
Perry, J. 2
Porcher, I. F. 112
Prechtl, J. C. 109

Queller, D. 84

Raymond, J. 94
Rees, G. 106
Roelofs, L. 27n.5
Russell, B.

Sainsbury, M. 40, 61n.21
Schacter, S 49
Schloss, K. 47–8

Seager, W. 27, 51n.12
Searle, J. 4–5
Sellars, W. 27–8, 91
Shewmon, A. 106–7
Shoemaker, S. 34, 73–4
Siewert, C. 65
Simon, J. 5
Singer, J. 49
Smart, J. J. C. 11–12
Smith, A. O. 41–2
Sneddon, L. 109n.4
Speaks, Jeff 39
Stoljar, D. 24, 34, 36, 63
Strassman, J. 84

Taylor, A. H. 107–8
Tononi, G. 8–9
Turner-Evans, D. 114
Tye, M. 5, 21–2, 32–3,
    32n.1, 38n.6, 39–41, 50n.11, 51n.12,
    54nn.14,15, 56, 63–6, 86n.10, 88n.12,
    90–1, 111

Van Gaal, S. 87
Van Gulick, R. 67n.24
Velleman, D. 63–4
Von Frisch, K. 113n.9

Watkins, S. 106
White, A. R. 36–7
Williamson, T. 4
Wright, C. 4

Yablo, S. 30n.6
Yamamoto, N. 109

Index

Note: Figures are indicated by an italic "*f*", respectively, following the page number.

For the benefit of digital users, indexed terms that span two pages (e.g., 52–53) may, on occasion, appear on only one of those pages.

2-D grid 8–9

adverbialism 34
all-or-nothing character 6
all-or-nothing phenomenon 4
animals 1–3, 21–2, 92–3, 107–16, 111n.5,
    see also bees, birds, dogs, fish, flies,
    insects, jellyfish, leeches, mammals,
    rats, sharks
anxiety 8, 112
arrays 48, 60–1
attend/attending 32–4, 36–8, 54–6, 63, 65,
    67–70, 67n.24, 72
attention 32, 36–8, 37n.4, 42–5, 52, 54, 62–3,
    65, 68–70, 76–7, 86
attentional blink 94
auditory
    commands 100–1
    cortex 107
    experience 43–4, 55–6
    perception 50
    sensations 14
awareness 35–8, 54–6, 62–3, 65, 71–2, 103,
    see also de re awareness, fact awareness,
    introspective awareness
awareness as 43–4, 56
awareness of 34–5, 43–4, 57–8, 62,
    66–7
awareness that 43–4, 56–7, 56n.17

bees 84, 112–14
behavioral
    concept 17
    control system 115
    definition 15, 17
    dispositions 19
    evidence 104, 112
    features 15, 17

impairment 104
outputs 7
properties 7
similarities 108–11
behaviorism 6
belief 5, 56n.17, 78–9, 83, 85–6, 92,
    105, 111
belief* 78–9
biological
    entities 92–3
    function 90–1
    waste 47–8
biologists 84
biology 16–17
birds 90–1, 107–9, 110*f*, 116
Blockhead 83
blur/blurriness 41–3, *see also*
    fuzzy/fuzziness
bodily
    arousal 49–50
    changes 48–50, 57–8
    damage 26n.2, 45, 47, 108–11, 114
    disturbances 44–8
    experiences 48, 50–2
    feelings, *see* feelings
    movements 82, 94–7, 101–2, 113
    sensations 43–8, 50–1, 55–8, 86
    states 49–50, 52, 57–8
    symptoms 48
    tissue, *see* tissue damage
Boodle's 82–3
borderline cases 1–2, 4–8, 13–18, 73, 76–9,
    89, 99
brain 1–3, 8–9, 11–12, 22, 24, 26–9, 61n.20,
    66, 87–8n.11, 88, 95, 100, 105, 107–11,
    115–16
    malformations 106
    processes 8, 113

brain (*cont.*)
  states 24–6, 28–30, 87–8, 95
  stem 102–6
  see also auditory cortex, cerebellum,
    cerebral cortex, cerebrum, claustrum,
    dorsal ventricular ridge, neocortex,
    occipital cortex, pallium, visual cortex

causal
  connection 3, 53
  difference 31, 95
  dispositions 19
  efficacy 2, 74–5, 93–9
  irrelevance 94–6
  power 93
  properties 19–20
  relation 53
  relevance 96–8
  roles 19
  tie 52
cerebellum 110*f*
cerebral cortex 103–4, 106
cerebrum 101*f*, 102*f*
China-body system 27n.5
claustrum 100–3, 101*f*, 102*f*, 105–9,
    111, 116
cognitive
  attention 36–7
  attitudes 37–8
  difference 85
  grasp 111n.5
  information 114
  poise 89–90, 92–3, 98–9
  processing 87
  psychologists 60
  reactions 105
  responses 87–90, 92, 112–13
color 4–5, 10, 26, 30, 32–3, 41–2, 47–8, 51,
    55, 58, 60–1, 63–72, 75–7, 79–80, 85–6,
    90–1, 105, 111n.5, 112–13
combination 19–20, 22, 28–9, 81
combination problem 2, 27, 74, 80–5,
    87–91
common phenomenal character 67, 71
conscious* 78–82, 85, 88–91, 93, 99n.17
consciousness* 2, 74–5, 78–85, 88–93,
    98–100
conscious states 2–3, 5, 8, 13, 15–17, 20–4,
    26, 28–30, 71–2, 74–9, 81, 87–93,
    95–9

conscious thoughts 50n.11, 54n.15, 55–8
constitution 95n.15, 97–8
content representationalism 39–40
cortex 87–8n.11, 100, 104, 108–9,
    110*f*, 116

datum 4, 34–5, *see also* sense-data,
    sense-datum theory
decorticate children 103–7, 111, 116
decorticate rats 104–5, 107, 111
delayed matching to sample (DMTS)
    112–13
delayed non-matching to sample
    (DNMTS) 112–13
de re awareness 33–5, 37–8, 43–4, 54–5,
    65–7, 71–2
de re cognitive attitudes 37–8
desire 83, 85–6, 92, 109–12
dogs 21–2, 46, 50
dopamine 8
dorsal ventricular ridge (DVR) 108–9
dualism 23–4, 29–31
dualists 11–12, 23–4, 29–31, 73–4, 95

electrical
  activity 101–2
  impulses 7
  rhythms 109
  shock 109–12
  signal 100–1
  stimulation 101–3, 105–6
electrons 11, 19–20, 22
electrophysiological responses 109
emotions 21–2, 48–55, 51n.12, 57–8,
    103–4
entities 3, 7, 11–12n.4, 15, 21–2,
    34–5, 37–8, 50, 64, 66, 74, 79–80,
    84–5, 87–8n.11, 88–90, 92–3,
    98–100, 99n.17
environment 15, 39, 43–4, 57
environmental
  events 103–4
  inputs 7
  relatedness 106
epiphenomenalism 95, 97
external
  body changes 50
  features 33
  objects 57–8
  particulars 33, 40, 56

properties 59
surface 64

fact awareness 34–5, 54–5, 57, 62, 66–7
feelings 5, 8, 13–14, 17, 20–2, 24–7, 44,
46–51, 54–6, 81, 86, 89–91, 102–4,
109–11
fish 107–12, 110f, 116, *see also* sharks
flies 114–15
Fregean content 40
functional
abnormalities 107
architecture 1
arrangement 84
arrays 61n.20
definition 15
features 15, 17
nature 10–11, 83
organization 89n.13
profile 107
properties 7, 9–11, 30, 78–9
relationship 106
roles 7–8, 112–13
states 1, 25–6, 28–9
types 24–5, 30
vision 106
functionalism 83–4
functionalist concept/theories 17, 73–4
fuzzy/fuzziness 4–5, 11–12n.4, 41–3, *see also*
blur/blurriness

global workspace 85–8, 99, 107, 111–13
global workspace theory (GWT) 87–9,
112–13
grounding 11, 28–30, *see also* metaphysical
grounding
gustatory experiences 43–4

hallucinations 33–4, 40, 44, 46, 53–5,
65–7
hallucinatory experiences 40, 53–4,
58, 71
Hegelian synthesis argument 23–5

identity 25, 95n.15
identity theory 6–7, 24, 28–9
illusions 33, 43–4, 108
illusory experiences 71
illusory perception 33
images/imagery 55–6, 60, 86

indeterminacy 2, 13–14, 76
information, *see* integrated information,
sensory information
informational properties 9
informational states 1, 26, 87
insects 21–2, 113–15, *see also* bees, flies
integrated information 8–9, 105–6, 114
intentional
action 97
features 34
object 52
stance 83
intentionality 63
internal
actions 96
bodily changes 50
bodily states 49
changes 52
nature 43–4
reports 57–8
states 56–7, 87, 89, 89n.13, 92–3
token states 97–9
intrinsic properties 23
introspectable
difference 39–40
qualities 71
states 86
introspection 32–6, 39, 42, 48, 54, 57–62,
64–5, 70, 72, 76–7
introspective awareness 5, 43–4,
54–8, 71
invasiveness 50–1

jellyfish 115–16

law of the excluded middle 6
leeches 115–16
light switch model 1–4
location of consciousness 100–16

macro-consciousness 2–3, 90
macro-conscious states 20, 22, 26, 28, 91
macro-phenomenal
properties 20, 28
states 24–7, 90–1
types 24–5, 28–9
macro-phenomenology 26–7, 91
mammals 87–8n.11, 104, 107–11,
110f, 114
matrix structure 60–1

memory 86, 100–1, 104–7, 112–13
mental
    chemistry 27–8
    entities 64
    facts 32, 71
    focus 63
    inexistence 65
    objects 64
    particulars 34–5
    phenomena 6
    property 83
    states 5, 54–6, 83–4, 86
meta-cognition 111n.5
metaphysical
    category of property 58
    grounding 9–11, 24–5, 28–30
    impossibility 16
    necessity 9–11, 25–6, 29–30,
        71n.26
    option 34–5
    possibility 15–16, 23–6, 31, 89, 98–9
metaphysics 59n.18
micro-entities 11–12n.4, 74, 99n.17
micro-experiences 27–8
micro-level 20, 24–5, 28–9, 31, 73, 81–2,
    89–90, 99n.17
microphenomenal properties 26
microphenomenal states 27
microphysical
    duplicates 89
    entities 3, 22, 79
    properties 10–11
    reality 2, 21
microphysics 8, 11–12n.4, 19–20, 74, 98–9
micro-quiddities 22–4, 29, 31, 91
micro-reality 2, 11–12n.4, 80
micro-realm 2, 74–5, 78–9
micro-subjects 27
missing ingredient 71–2
moods 21–2, 48–58

neocortex 100, 103, 108, 111
neural
    architecture 1
    basis of consciousness 105
    configurations 12
    constitution 97–8
    maps 103
    properties 7, 30, 97–8
    states 1, 95

neurological
    complexity 2, 77
    states 1
    type 29
neurologists 106
neuronal activity 105
neuronal oscillation 6–7
neurons 6–7, 12, 95, 100, 105–8, 114–16
neurophysiological
    evidence 111
    processes 31
    properties 7
    types 25
neurophysiology 8, 31
nociceptors 109–12
nomological dangler 12

occipital cortex 106–7
olfactory experiences/sense 43–4, 112–13
organisms 17, 21–2, 84–5, *see also*
    superorganisms
origin of the universe 11

pain 5, 13–14, 20, 24–8, 44–7, 77–8, 81, 86,
    89–91, 103–4, 108–12, 114–15
pallium 109, 110*f*
panpsychism 2, 21, 27n.3, 73–5
panpsychist representationalism 80, 99
panpsychists 2, 21, 74
panpsychist view 2, 22
paradox 2, 4, 6, 24–5, 28–31, 34, 72–5,
    78–80, 99
    explained 6–18
perception 36, 36n.3, 39, 48–50, 56, 62–5, 67, 100
    of bodily changes 48–50
    see also auditory perception, illusory
        perception, visual perception
perceptual experiences 34, 39n.7, 43–4, 48,
    50–1, 54n.15, 55–6, 87–8
phenomenal
    causation 34, 36, 39–40, 47, 58–9, 67–71,
        79–80, 96–7
    consciousness 5–6, 14–15, 72, 80
    experiences 39–41, 58, 71, 75, 80
    memory image 86
    pinkness 27–8, 91
    properties 28, 95–7
    quiddities 20–7, 29–31, 74, 91
    states 24, 31, 75, 90, 95
    variation 76–7

phenomenal-physical laws 11–12, 23–4, 29–30
phenomenology 5, 14–15, 26–8, 44, 49–50, 55–6, 63, 91
physical
    account of consciousness 8–9
    behavior 97
    changes 48–9
    complexes 84–5, 99
    dimensions 49–50
    domain 99
    duplicates 23
    entities 7, 74
    features 26
    inputs and outputs 7
    laws 11–12, 19–20, 22–4, 29–30
    objects 64
    phenomenon 6, 8, 73
    properties 1, 8–12, 29–30, 47, 79–80, 94–5, 97, 99
    reality 73, 91, 98–9
    sciences 9, 11, 19–20, 31, 95
    states 12–13, 88, 95
    structures 11–12, 99, 111
physicalism 22–5, 27, 29–30, 74, 88
physicalist
    accounts of consciouness 22
    metaphysical grounding 10
    theories 73–4
    views 22–4, 26
physicalists 2, 6, 11, 23, 73–4
physics 3, 19–20
poise 85–90, 92–3, 98–9
prefrontal cortex (PFC) 105–7, 116
primitivist Russellian Monism (RM) 24, 28–30
    objections 28–31
projectivism 64
property representationalism 39, 58–62, 69–71
property representationalists 40, 59, 67, 70
proto-phenomenal properties 20
psychological experiments 27–8, 49, 93
psychological subjects 27, 93, see also tiny psychological subjects

qualia 32–3, 59, 63–4, 69, 70n.25, 71
qualia realism 34–9, 64, 67, 69–70
qualia realists 37, 56, 59, 63, 71

quantum entanglement 3
quantum mechanics 11–12n.4
quarks 21–2, 26, 76–9, 81–2, 90–1, 93, 100
quiddities 20, 22, 28, 30, 73, 89, 98, see also micro-quiddities, phenomenal quiddities

rats 16n.7, 104–5, 107, 111, 114, 116
reality 11–12n.4, 19–20, 68, 70, 74, see also microphysical reality, micro-reality, physical reality
reductive Russellian Monism (RM) 24–30
    objections 25–8
relational/structural properties of matter 19, 74
representationalism 32–77, 79–80, see also content representationalism, panpsychist representationalism, property representationalism
Rubik's cube 81
Russellian Monism (RM) 11, 19, 22–4, 27–8, 30n.6, 31, 89
    objections 2, 31
    versions 24–5
    see also primitivist Russellian Monism, reductive Russellian Monism
Russellian monists 19–24, 27, 30, 31n.8, 74, 91

sensations 13–14, 32–5, 45–6, 71, see also auditory sensations, bodily sensations
sense-data 51, 64
sense-datum theory 34, 64
sensory
    attention 36–7
    experience 21–2, 50
    information 109, 112–13
    input 115
    modalities 106
    motor coupling 114
    motor modules 113
    neurons 7, 105
    receptors 48–9
    representation 65–6, 113
serotonin 8
sharks 112, 114
smells 43–4, 51, 105, 113
soul 25–6

spatiotemporal properties 19–20
split brain subjects 27–8
superorganisms 84
supervenience thesis 71n.26

tactual experiences 43–4
tiny psychological subjects 2, 74, 91–3
tissue damage 45, 47, 109–11
transparency 31–41, 43–8, 45n.9, 54, 63–5, 67–9, 72, 79–80
transparency thesis 32–4, 39, 41, 43, 62
type identity theory 6–7

undirected consciousness 2, 74–80

vision 41–2, 57–8, 60, 106–7, 113
visual
    awareness 63

commands 100–1
cortex 7, 105, 107
experiences 13, 24, 27, 32–44, 53–4, 57–62, 67, 79–81, 85–6, 91, 95–6
illusions 108
landmarks 113–14
perception 33–4, 105–6
phenomenology 63
qualities 66
state 93–7
stimuli 87, 103–4
system 93–4, 106
vitalists 17

water 11
working memory 105–7, 112–13

zombies 15, 23–5, 31, 89, 98–9